941.083

D0119716

Junior Library
Cheltenham
Ladies' College

ACC NO : 18418-7   909.82
TITLE   : BRITAIN IN THE 1930s

AUTHOR : FREEMAN CHARLES

DDC(1) : 941.083

3867

Living Through History

BRITAIN IN THE 1930S

CHARLES FREEMAN

Batsford Academic and Educational
London

ACKNOWLEDGMENTS

The Author and Publishers thank the following for their kind permission to reproduce copyright illustrations: Aerofilms Ltd, figure 48; BBC Hulton Picture Library, figures 4, 6, 11, 14, 15, 16, 17, 29, 34, 38, 40, 41, 43, 47, 49, 54, 55, 58, 60; Communist Party Picture Library, figures 37, 53, 56; The Electricity Council, figure 5; Illustrated London News Picture Library, figure 42; Keystone Press Agency Ltd, figures 7, 30; National Museum of Labour History, figures 31, 33, 39; National Portrait Gallery, figures 8, 21, 35; Popperfoto, figures 20, 27; Punch Publications Ltd, figure 12; The Telecom Technology Showcase, London, figure 52; TUC Library, figures 3, 22; University College London Library (George Orwell Archive), figure 36; Wiener Library, figures 1, 28. The pictures were researched by Alexandra Wiessler.

Cover pictures
The colour picture on the front cover shows "Dance-Time at the Dorchester Hotel" from *The By-Stander*, 3 June 1931 (The Illustrated London News Picture Library). The portrait is of Nye Bevan. The right-hand picture shows the Jarrow March (Beamish North of England Open Air Museum).

© Charles Freeman 1985
First published 1985

All rights reserved. No part of this publication
may be reproduced, in any form or by any means,
without permission from the Publisher

Typeset by Tek-Art Ltd, Kent
and printed in Great Britain by
R.J. Acford
Chichester, Sussex
for the publishers
Batsford Academic and Educational,
an imprint of B.T. Batsford Ltd,
4 Fitzhardinge Street
London W1H 0AH

ISBN 0 7134 4354 5

CONTENTS

THE ILLUSTRATIONS

THE 1930s

"A low dishonest decade": this is how the poet W.H. Auden, writing in exile in the United States on 1 September 1939, summed up the 1930s. On the very day he was writing these words in New York, the armed forces of Nazi Germany were sweeping across the borders of Poland. Two days later Britain and France, honouring their promises to support Poland, declared war on Germany. For Europe the Second World War had begun.

The failure to play a constructive role in keeping peace in Europe was perhaps the most serious failure of British politics in the 1930s. The impact of the First World War had been so shattering that few believed that any politician would ever run the risk again of leading their country into war. Many believed that for Europe war was now a thing of the past and that little effort would be needed to maintain peace. As Leonard Woolf, the political journalist, put it in his Introduction to *The Intelligent Man's Way to Prevent War* (1934),

1 German troops stream into Poland, September 1939, shattering hopes of lasting peace in Europe.

2 For many, radio broadcasts were one of the miracles of the age. Here a family in a remote part of the country tune in to the national news.

[war] is preventable in Europe like cannibalism, cholera or witchcraft, all of which have been abolished by civilisation. . . . Any intelligent person can, with a little trouble, understand the problem of preventing war. Though it is not a simple problem, it is not nearly so complicated as that of making a six-cylinder engine for a motor car and it is child's play compared to the intricate mass of problems which have been solved to make broadcasting possible.

Such hopes were to be dashed by the rise and expansion of Nazi Germany, a political force which glorified war and conquest. The threat posed by Germany was seen only dimly and belatedly by the majority of British politicians and their reactions to it were timid and makeshift. The failure to prevent German aggression meant that in 1939 Britain found herself at war again. In this sense, the 1930s was a profoundly depressing decade and Auden's pessimism is not surprising.

Another depressing feature of the decade was the prevalence of mass unemployment. There had never been a period in British history in which unemployment had been so widespread or persistent. In early 1933 there were over three million out of work and, despite some recovery over the decade, the

figure always remained over one million. Unemployment was worst in the centres of Britain's traditional export industries, coal-mining, shipbuilding and cotton. These industries had first been hit by foreign competition after the First World War and then by the collapse of world trade during the Great Depression of 1929 to 1933. Britain had launched 1.4 million tons of shipping in 1930. In 1933 the figure was 133,000 tons. Cotton exports which had been 7,000 million yards in 1913 were down to 2,000 million in 1937.

In areas which depended heavily on these industries the effects were catastrophic. South Wales was perhaps the worst hit of the mining areas. The valleys fell silent as the pits closed and the many fine choirs and rugby teams were disbanded. Even in 1935 50 per cent of

4 An unemployed Newcastle family return home, March 1939. Unemployment figures remained high until the end of the decade.

3 Unemployment reached its peak in the early thirties. Here a group of shipyard lads from Glasgow wait around for employment.

the population were out of work in some towns. The great shipbuilding areas such as Clydeside and Tyneside were equally badly affected.

Unemployment did much to take the heart out of traditional working-class communities. The response, however, was not revolution but apathy. Many unemployed assumed that the Depression was a force over which they, their employers, or even the government, had little control. George Orwell, writing of Wigan, reported "the frightful feeling of impotence and despair which is almost the worst evil of unemployment". The "dole", or unemployment benefit, did give some protection where in earlier pre-war depressions there had been none and in some cases it was actually more generous than wages. Private charity helped to supplement the dole and some historians have even argued that more was given out through local charities than through state schemes.

The greatest bitterness of the unemployed was directed against the administration of benefits. All insured workers had the right to six months' benefit if they became unemployed. After that they were made subject to a Means Test before further assistance could be given. The Means Test took into account savings, possessions and the income of other members of the family. The intrusion into the home and the prying questions involved were deeply resented and with a million of the unemployed subject to the Test by 1932 this has been seen as one of the few issues on which genuine revolutionary feeling might have been built. As an illustration, when the famous Jarrow marchers left Jarrow to walk south with their petition to Parliament for work, they found that their unemployment benefit was automatically stopped because they were not available in Jarrow if work had become available.

What was perhaps extraordinary was how these communities, though depressed, did manage to keep together and maintain their traditional values. Stephen Constantine in his *Unemployment in Britain between the Wars* sums up his study of the effects of unemployment as follows:

Working people seem to have been extraordinarily resilient or stubborn in the face of depression. Communities did not break up; there was migration but no mass exodus from the depressed areas. Unemployment brought poverty into many homes and physical and mental suffering too often accompanied it. But established patterns of working class politics survived; attitudes to work, values in the family, respect for law and order and political behaviour were not substantially altered.

Pictures of the unemployed so dominate our impressions of the 1930s that it is easy to forget that, overall, the decade was one of solid recovery. While many communities were devastated by unemployment, many more experienced steady growth and even prosperity. It was as if there were two Britains that never met, though younger workers did migrate from the depressed areas to the more affluent ones. The facts were clear. Britain's growth rate in the thirties was 1.8 per cent a year in comparison to 1.7 per cent a year in Roosevelt's America. While Britain's industrial production was 20 per cent higher

5 In the 1930s a wide variety of electrical goods spread to middle-class homes. Here a mother shows off a new fridge. Note too the electric cooker in the background.

6   The dream of the city dweller – a home in the sub-urbs complete with garage and motor car.

in 1938 than it had been in 1929, France's was 24 per cent *lower*. The average Briton was 15 per cent better-off at the end of the decade than he was at the beginning.

This improvement was most evident in the expansion of new industries. By 1933 Britain had established a national electricity grid, "one of the most advanced systems of electricity supply in the world" (Stevenson and Cook, *The Slump*), and supplies quickly spread to private homes, one third of which had electricity by 1930 and two thirds by the end of the decade. Employment in the industry doubled and the market for electrical appliances grew. Under 38,000 vacuum cleaners were made in 1930, over 400,000 in 1935.

The number of private cars grew steadily – there were one million on the roads in 1930, two million by 1939. A middle-class family could hope to own one by the end of the decade. Here was employment not only on the production lines, but for garages, roadbuilders and all who could make a living out of the passing traffic. The expansion was haphazard. There were few rules or regulations before the 1930s and not surprisingly casualties were high – over 7,000 deaths a year and 100,000 injured. Altogether, it is estimated that 120,000 died and one and a half million were injured on the roads in the twenties and thirties. Gradually, speed limits, zebra crossings, roundabouts and driving tests were introduced and the casualty rates dropped. There is no doubt that the opportunities opened up by the spread of cheap motor transport were enormous.

As it became easy to move raw materials around by road and as electricity, rather than coal, became the main form of energy, it was possible for new industries to break away from the traditional industrial areas. This is one reason why these areas did not share in the return to prosperity. Factories were now built near the consumers. Between 1932 and 1937 80 per cent of new factories and two thirds of new employment were created in the London area and it is along the main roads out of the capital that we can still best study the architecture of the period.

The thirties, in fact, were a great age of building. Three million new homes were built in the decade. While in 1917 there had been 610,000 *fewer* homes than families, by 1938 there were 500,000 *more*. Much of the building was of middle-class suburbs. These have been ridiculed by many. A.J.P. Taylor in his *English History 1914-45*, for instance, writes:

These new settlements had no centres, no sense, no communal spirit. They were composed of little more than individual motor cars come to rest.

George Orwell is even more scathing: in *Coming Up For Air* (1939) he describes

the stucco fronts, the creosoted gate, the privet hedge, the green front door, the Laurels, the Myrtles, the Hawthorns, Mon Abri, Mon Repos, Belle Vue. At perhaps one house in fifty, some anti-social type who will probably end in the workhouse has painted his front door blue instead of green.

Whatever the sterility of many of these estates, however, the chance to own property, to have space, to be mobile and to escape the damp of many older homes was a vital and important social development.

It was not only the middle classes who benefited from the new building. With a down payment of £25 for a semi-detached house which would cost a total of £450, the more prosperous members of the working class could afford their own homes. Under an Act passed by the Labour Government in 1930, a programme of extensive slum clearance got under way. Only 17,000 slum homes had been demolished in the 1920s; in the 1930s over a million slum dwellers were rehoused. Many overcrowded homes remained, but a significant start had been made. The new council housing was a major improvement on the old. In York, where forty to fifty houses had originally been built to the acre, the new council estates averaged twelve.

In health, housing and food there were improvements during these years. To take one instance, infant mortality had been 110 per 1000 in 1911-15; twenty years later it was down to 62. Spending on social services, which had taken up a third of government expenditure in 1913, took up 46 per cent of a much larger budget in 1933. Paul Addison in *The Road to 1945* claims: "The social services in Britain, taken all in all, were the most advanced in the world in 1939." There remained, however, significant gaps, patched together inadequately by private charity.

For the majority of the population, therefore, life was becoming easier. There was more leisure, more entertainment, both from the cinema where the "talkies" were firmly established and from the radio which had reached most homes by 1939. There was much greater opportunity to travel. In 1931 only one and a half million people were eligible for paid holidays; by 1939 the figure was eleven million. This was a great age for the seaside resort. The first Butlin's opened in 1937. Cycling and hiking were enormously popular.

These steady improvements and the consolidation of middle-class life that they brought with them do much to explain the extraordinary stability and conservatism of British society in these years. Those who preached revolutionary change were a tiny minority who made virtually no impact on the electorate. In London a glittering society life continued, described by one observer as consisting of six hundred people who all knew each other and much of what was going on between each other but who successfully kept this knowledge from the outside world. Their activities are vividly described in the diaries of Chips Channon (see pages 48-51). The middle classes led a more sober life and one of solid good order. In *Still Life*, Richard Cobb describes the life of middle-class Tunbridge Wells:

Every person in his or her place, every object in its place, the whole town breathing regularly to a

predictable timetable, everything as it should be, a place that was safe and cherished and remembered as such.

The monarchy retained great prestige and appears to have had the support of all classes. George V, King from 1910 to 1936, seems to have been genuinely surprised at the affection in which he was held and his Jubilee celebrations of 1935 were a huge success. A common sight in the poorer streets of his kingdom were posters inscribed "Lousy [i.e. suffering from lice] but Loyal". His son, Edward, Prince of Wales, appeared to show real interest in the problems of the unemployed, visiting many of the depressed areas. It was Edward, however, who was to provide the major domestic crisis of the decade. Coming to the throne aged over forty and unmarried, he was already deeply involved with Mrs Wallis Simpson, a twice-married American. His determination to marry her led to a head-on clash with his government and finally, in December 1936, Edward was forced to abdicate. His brother, who came to the throne as George VI, was more shy and less flamboyant than Edward, but with the help of his highly popular Queen (now the Queen Mother), he restored the prestige and popularity of the Crown.

7 The Royal Family remained the focus of national loyalty. George VI receives the cheers of the crowds after his Coronation in May 1937. With him are his Queen, Elizabeth, now the Queen Mother, and his two daughters, the present Queen and Princess Margaret.

The politicians of this period were content to preserve the fabric of British life. Just at a time when Britain became a full democracy (all women were eligible to vote for the first time in the 1929 election), power seemed to be consolidated in fewer hands. The politicians of the National Government (see page 13), with their enormous majorities during the thirties, had little to fear from opposition. "More and more," wrote Chips Channon in the late thirties, and it seems approvingly, "we are being ruled by a small group of thirty to forty people." Neville Chamberlain, Prime Minister from 1937-40, carried out his foreign policy with little reference to anyone. The BBC, an increasingly important influence, consistently supported government policies, often censoring attacks on them.

Most of the leading politicians of the decade had been born into a very different age. Ramsay MacDonald, Prime Minister in the Labour Government of 1929-31 and the National Government of 1931-5, was in serious decline and by the time he retired was an isolated and pathetic figure. He was succeeded by the Conservative leader, Stanley Baldwin, now Prime Minister for the third time at sixty-seven. Baldwin was succeeded two years later by Neville Chamberlain, already aged sixty-eight. These men had all been born in the 1860s. They had grown up in a world where Britain was dominant and in which steady and solid prosperity seemed assured. In their forties, this world had been shattered by the First World War; in their sixties, they were faced with the challenge of the Great Depression. It was not surprising that they found it difficult to adapt to the new age. Oswald Mosley, the fascist leader, and thirty years younger, was quick to taunt them as representatives of a vanished world, one which his movement was ready to displace (see pages 18-22).

These British leaders were increasingly conscious of the vulnerability of Britain, still head of an enormous Empire, at a time of economic disarray. They were bewildered by new political forces such as Bolshevism in Russia and fascism in Germany and Italy. Such political movements had little in common with the leisured and tolerant British approach to politics. Their response was, above all, one of caution and there is little evidence that the British electorate demanded or wanted anything else. These facts do much to explain the solid but unimaginative government that Britain experienced in the thirties. The most brilliant and forceful politician of these years, Winston Churchill seemed, in fact, to belong to an age even earlier than that of Baldwin and Chamberlain.

Nor did the Labour Party offer much of a challenge to the political system in these years. The left in Britain had suffered many setbacks. It had been defeated in the General Strike of 1926, the Labour Government of 1929-31 had collapsed in the face of the Depression and the Parliamentary Labour Party had done disastrously in the election of 1931. In Europe as a whole, the left was in retreat – in Austria, in Nazi Germany and fascist Italy and in Spain where the Republican cause was finally extinguished in 1939. The Labour Party was confused, the trade union movement, subdued by the experience of mass unemployment, was cautious. The leaders of the Party realized there was no depth of revolutionary feeling on which to build and they played little part in the hunger marches and other demonstrations of the period. In a conservative age their only hope was to capture the middle ground, but the Conservative leader, Stanley Baldwin, held this securely.

Extremist parties remained small. There was a brief flowering of British fascism, but the movement never seemed likely to find roots in Britain and, in fact, never even contested a General Election. The Communists, likewise, achieved virtually no support. At the height of the Depression, in the election of 1931, the Party's 26 candidates polled only 74,000 votes between them. In 1935, one candidate, Willie Gallacher, was elected, for West Fife in Scotland, but the total number of votes cast for Communism was even smaller, at 27,000. The Party had only 9,000 members in 1932.

During these years Britain still was the ruler of a vast Empire, but there was a growing acceptance that her role as an imperial power was changing. In 1931 the Statute of Westminster recognized the complete independence from control by the British Parliament of the Dominions: Canada, Australia, South Africa and New Zealand.

The great jewel of the British Empire remained India. This highly complex nation with its Princes, its many races and religions was still controlled by a small elite of British administrators and soldiers. British rule was usually competent, but it was increasingly vulnerable to attack from politically aware Indians, on grounds of racism, exploitation and, on occasions such as the Amritsar Massacre of 1919, cruelty. There were growing demands for increased Indian participation in government and eventual independence. The debates over India were, in fact, to dominate Parliamentary life in the early 1930s and it was only after a long and bitter struggle that the Government of India Act was passed in 1935. It was one step on to

India's eventual independence in 1947.

By the late 1930s foreign affairs of a very different kind dominated the headlines. When the Italian dictator, Mussolini, invaded Abyssinia in 1935, there was genuine outrage among the British public, but the government handled the crisis badly, failing to use the League of Nations, of which Britain was a leading member, to make an effective stand against the invasion. Only a year later the Spanish Civil War broke out. "Spain was not so much a place as the name of a cause," writes Samuel Hynes in *The Auden Generation*. To the left in Britain, as elsewhere in Europe, it seemed that this was the vital struggle where freedom had to be defended against the forces of fascism. Many left to fight and some died. The eventual defeat of the Republic was for many on the left the most depressing event of the decade.

It was the problem of Germany, however, which was to prove the most perplexing. Few welcomed the rise of Hitler or Nazism. The excesses of the regime were too widely publicized for that. The question remained: Did Hitler offer a long-term threat to Britain? Were his aims limited, confined, for instance, to rectifying the more humiliating clauses of the Treaty of Versailles, made at the end of the First World War and recognized by many in Britain to have been unnecessarily harsh? In this case, his demands could be met by negotiation. Or was he bent on world conquest? If so, what could a poorly armed Britain, with a large and vulnerable Empire, do about it? This was the dilemma that faced the British politicians of the late thirties. They chose negotiations and were proved wrong. (See the biographies of Churchill and Chamberlain.)

As the news from Europe became steadily more gloomy, those who were committed to playing a creative role for peace and freedom found it hard to know how to react. Many must have felt as the writer John Lehmann did in 1935: "How to find sanity and clear thought again. How to defend oneself. How to be active, not to crouch paralysed as the hawk descends."

In many ways, Britain in the 1930s gives a picture of being "paralysed as the hawk descends". Her leaders were haunted by memories of the last war and the Depression from which the nation was slowly recovering. They were so concerned with maintaining stability at home (not that it was ever seriously threatened) that they had no energy or will to play a creative role abroad. "A low dishonest decade" may be too harsh a criticism of the 1930s. Government was certainly competent, if often bureaucratic and narrow. It was not a time of social disintegration. However, the final and most important challenge of all, the maintenance of international peace with justice was never faced with the creative energy the task deserved.

POLITICIANS

In 1929, for the second time in British history, a Labour Government achieved power.

"At long last England has arisen and the day is here, the new day when the people of Britain shall come into their own," rejoiced the veteran Labour MP George Lansbury.

Within a few months these high hopes had been dashed. With the Wall Street Crash of 1929, world trade slumped. Britain, still a great trading nation, was hard hit, and her traditional industries, already disrupted by the First World War, collapsed further. Unemployment rose from 1.7 million in late 1929 to 2.7 million by mid-1931.

The Labour Party had often talked of such a collapse of capitalism. Now the collapse had come, they had few ideas as to how to deal with it. The Labour leader, Ramsay MacDonald, believed in the traditional remedy of balancing the budget, making sure that the government spent no more than it received in taxes. In fact, this meant that he had to cut government spending. One of the main items of spending was unemployment benefits, desperately needed by those thrown out of work.

Not surprisingly, many members of MacDonald's government refused to make such cuts. MacDonald was not to be deterred. In August 1931, with strong support from the King, George V, he decided to form a new National Government, composed of all those from the main political parties who would support him. The mass of Labour members refused to join.

In October 1931, MacDonald called a General Election. The National Government won easily, with 556 seats against a tiny 46 for the Labour Party that MacDonald had deserted. His victory, however, was a hollow one. Only 13 former members of his party supported him in Parliament and the 472 Conservatives who made up the mass of the Government's supporters had very little respect for him. MacDonald was to continue as Prime Minister until 1935, but he was no longer an effective leader and he became an ever more pathetic and isolated figure in these years.

Although they kept the name "National Government", the governments of these years were dominated by the Conservative Party. They faced no serious political threat throughout the decade from any other party or political movement. Britain made a slow recovery from the Depression and the general mood of the country seemed to be for stability and caution. Perhaps the political figure who most reflected this mood in the 1930s was Stanley Baldwin.

Stanley Baldwin (1867-1947)

It is hard to think of a politician who more responded to the hopes and fears of the British middle classes in these years than did Stanley Baldwin, Prime Minister between 1935 and 1937. At a time of economic depression, national self-doubt and increasing international tension, Baldwin gave the message which the nation most wanted to hear. Everything would be all right and the British virtues of common sense, decency and

8 Stanley Baldwin, a typical pose complete with pipe.

thence to the post of Prime Minister, in 1923, but the qualities for which he was recommended to the King, "honesty, simplicity and balance", had much to do with it. He was appointed over the head of the more obvious choice, the brilliant but aloof Lord Curzon. Almost at once, Baldwin fell from power, but was returned as Prime Minister in 1924 and held the post until 1929.

Baldwin's genius as a politician lay in his ability to portray himself as the representative of the deepest needs and feelings of the nation. His handling of the General Strike of 1926 was masterly. What appeared at first to be a clash of classes, splitting British society down the centre, was transformed by Baldwin into an attack by the strikers on the British constitution itself. Having thus discredited the strike in the eyes of many, he tried to settle it with moderation. Many in the workers' movements were never to forgive him for his approach, but it made him appear the saviour of middle-class England.

Baldwin's whole image reflected his views: his pipe, his slightly plump figure, his clothes, well-made, homely, but never too formal, his air of benign feeling for his fellow men. Younger politicians testified to him as the nicest man in politics. Even members of the

tolerance would pull the country through. He saw Britain as the British liked to see themselves, an industrial nation, maybe, but one rooted in rural traditions, a nation which avoided extremes and which valued peace, stability and good sense.

Baldwin, an only child, was born in 1867. His father was the successful owner of the family ironworks in Worcestershire, an excellent businessman but a stern father who was never close to his son. Baldwin's mother was an invalid and he must have had a lonely childhood. A need for affection seems to have remained with him for the rest of his life.

He followed his father into the family business, but his heart was never in it and he eventually became an MP in 1908, taking over the Conservative seat his father had occupied. There was nothing at the time to mark him out from the mass of Conservative MPs – he spoke only five times in his first six years in Parliament.

However, he was a likable and solid man and these qualities were eventually recognized and rewarded. This is not the place for the story of his sudden and unexpected rise to leadership of the Conservative Party, and

9 A cigarette card of the period, one of a series on political figures.

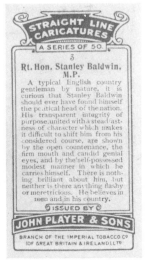

Labour opposition warmed to him. Clement Attlee, leader of the Labour Party from 1935, said, "I always felt that although he disagreed with us, he understood better than any man on the other [i.e. Conservative] side the reasons and emotions that inspired our actions."

Baldwin claimed that it was, in the last resort, his Christian faith which governed his actions and strengthened his beliefs. Speaking in May 1928, he told the British and Foreign Bible Society,

If I did not feel that our work . . . was done in the faith and hope that at some day, it may be a million years hence, the Kingdom of God would spread over the whole world, I could have no hope, I could do no work and I would give over my office to anyone who would take it.

He also talked of the eternal truths to be found in the traditional patterns of English country life. In a famous speech he dwelt on

the sounds of England, the tinkle of the hammer on the anvil in the country smithy, the corncrake on a dewy morning, the sound of the scythe against a whetstone and the sight of a ploughteam coming across the brow of a hill, the sight that has been seen in England since England was a land and may be seen in England long after the Empire has perished and every works in England has ceased to function, for centuries the one eternal sight of England.

Such visions of eternal peace were certainly welcome to many who were bewildered in the troubled years of the thirties, but the emphasis was wrong. These were the years when

10 The Indian nationalist leader, Mahatma Gandhi visited Britain in 1931 to discuss moves towards Indian independence. Here he is visiting Lancashire textile firms who feared the loss of their Indian markets.

thoughts needed to be directed towards industrial recovery and the threat of fascism – not the peace of the countryside.

Despite his outward appearance of calm and unflappability, Baldwin was, in fact, often nerve-wracked and unsure of himself. He seldom took the lead on issues himself, preferring to wait until he could sense what others were feeling and then respond to that feeling. In the first years of the National Government, when Baldwin was Lord President of the Council, a close friend of his, Thomas Jones, recorded, "Being second and not first suits him perfectly and frees him from the final decision and therefore the worry." At times when firm leadership was needed – for instance, during his third term of office, the Abyssinian crisis of 1935-6 – Baldwin failed to provide it. Throughout his life, he would respond to pressure by withdrawing, often on holiday in France, far removed from the political battlefield.

During his third term of office, Baldwin presided over a gradual recovery from economic depression. The recovery was hardly due to the actions of the National Government. There had been few measures which had either stimulated the economy or provided comprehensive help for those who were hardest hit. Nevertheless, Baldwin was too clever a politician to miss his chance and he was able to sell the recovery as the result of his government's stable rule. Few found themselves able to challenge him.

There were, however, important issues on which Baldwin did exercise his influence with success. The major parliamentary battle of the early thirties was over the future of India. Indian calls for independence had been gathering strength and the situation there had been dramatized worldwide by the non-violent campaigns of Gandhi. Baldwin himself had never been to India, but was a close friend of Lord Irwin (later Lord Halifax) who had been Viceroy there. Irwin was convinced that progress had to be made towards Indian self-rule and Baldwin came to agree with him:

What have we taught India for a century? We have maintained English institutions and democracy and all the rest of it. We have taught her the lesson and she wants us to pay the bill. There is a wind of nationalism and freedom blowing around the world and blowing as strongly in Asia as anywhere in the world . . . we should have failed in one of our main imperial understandings if we were not able to extend the field of self-government in India.

It was not only these beliefs that inspired Baldwin's views on India. He recognized that Britain was becoming over-extended and sensed that the British people realized this too. As Francis Williams, a journalist in the thirties, wrote, "His instinct was right, he could smell the change of climate of opinion among the ordinary people of Britain, weary of the responsibilities of imperial power."

Baldwin's main opponents were within the Conservative Party itself. A small group of the so-called diehards, brilliantly led by Winston Churchill, refused to contemplate the loss of British power. It was to be a bitter struggle,

11 The relationship between Edward, Prince of Wales and Mrs Simpson was well-known to London society but not to the general public. Here they are together at Ascot in 1935.

12 Stanley Baldwin retired in May 1937. A *Punch* cartoon (26 May 1937) shows John Bull (England) congratulating him on the steadiness of his work. Baldwin always saw his values as rooted in those of the countryside.

THE WORCESTERSHIRE LAD

FARMER BULL. "WELL DONE, STANLEY: A LONG DAY AND A RARE STRAIGHT FURROW."

both inside and outside of Parliament, before the 1935 Government of India Act was passed and India took a further step towards the independence which was to come to her only twelve years later. It was to Baldwin's credit that he set his ideals and maintained them in the bitter struggle over the passing of the Act.

The most embarrassing and delicate issue facing Baldwin in his third term of office was the Abdication crisis. The King, Edward VIII, who had succeeded his father in January 1936, was deeply involved with Wallis Simpson, a twice-married American. The affair was widely known in the close-knit society life of London and talked of freely in the overseas press, but kept for many months from the mass of British people. The crisis came to a head in October 1936 when Mrs Simpson began divorce proceedings against her second husband. Baldwin realized that this was the first step to make her legally free to marry the King. He went to see Edward and told him that the British people would not accept such a marriage. "I think I know our people. They will tolerate a lot in private life but they will not stand for this sort of thing in a public personage". In this, Baldwin was right. Many felt that he had misjudged public opinion but when the affair became public and MPs went off to consult their constituents, they found it was as he had said. Baldwin also had strong support from the Church, the leaders of the other political parties and the governments of Australia and New Zealand. When Edward refused to give way, he was forced to abdicate.

In the House of Commons in December 1936, Baldwin told the whole story.

To a quiet and attentive house he made one of his greatest speeches. It lasted just under an hour, a triumph of art that concealed art, that gave the King the most favourable interpretation at each stage of the tangled skein of events and which lifted the crisis at last from rumour and scandal on to the high dramatic plane where it has since largely remained. (Barnes and Middlemas, *Baldwin*)

As one MP, Harold Nicolson wrote in his diary:

We file out broken in body and soul, conscious that we have heard the best speech we shall ever hear in our lives. No man has ever dominated the House as he dominated it today and he knows it.

When Baldwin retired a few months later, it was, again in Nicolson's words, "in a blaze of affection".

Sadly, such national affection was not to last. As the true nature of Hitler's war plans became known, Baldwin was increasingly blamed for not warning the nation earlier of the threats which Hitler presented. Affection turned to ridicule, even hatred from some. Seldom has a political reputation been so quickly shattered by the unfolding of history.

Baldwin, with others, must share the

blame. He was always, first and foremost, a domestic politician and he never gave sufficient time and thought to foreign affairs. He depended, perhaps too heavily, on his continuing relationship with the British middle class and he became reluctant to break that relationship even when the needs of the nation required it. He freely admitted that it was the pressure of public opinion which kept him from speeding up the efforts to rearm. In this respect, perhaps, he failed to be a great leader, one who could set new visions and persuade others to create them.*

*This is perhaps too harsh a judgement. Robert Rhodes James in *The British Revolution* argues that Baldwin, in fact, took a prominent part in encouraging rearmament.

As a result of his change in fortunes, Baldwin's last years were unhappy ones. Tom Jones, his old friend, visited him and his wife in 1945 and found "their loneliness and separation from friends complete". Baldwin's wife died in 1945 and he himself in 1947.

Despite the shadows cast over his last years, Baldwin remains one of the most attractive of British Prime Ministers. His qualities were real and lasting. He maintained an atmosphere of tolerance and moderation at the centre of British political life, which was in marked contrast to the bitterness found in continental politics of the decade. His mistake was to believe that Britain could be isolated from that bitterness.

Oswald Mosley (1896-1980)

One of the most extraordinary political figures of the 1930s was Oswald Mosley, leader of the British Union of Fascists. In many ways, Mosley was one of the most gifted men of his generation. He was an intellectual with strong and original ideas, a fine speaker and a man of enormous energy with impressive sporting achievements. He was one of the few politicians of his time who tried to create new visions of the future. Sadly, with all these gifts, Mosley was an unstable and restless person, with little sense of what was politically possible. When he felt that his gifts had not been recognized by the traditional political parties, he left them and tried to build a fascist movement to replace them. It was a fatal political miscalculation and ended with Mosley becoming a political and social outcast.

Mosley was born in 1896, the eldest son of a Staffordshire baronet. However, he saw little of his father, "a hard-riding, hard-drinking, traditional Tory squire" and was brought up mainly by his mother, a determined woman who adored and spoiled him. He was, from the start, "a solitary, imaginative boy prone to day-dreaming and introspection" (Robert Skidelsky, *Oswald Mosley*). This sense of loneliness lasted all his life. However, he had both energy and skill. He became, at fifteen, the youngest ever public schools fencing champion. When war broke out in 1914, he avoided the aristocratic cavalry regiments and became a member of the Royal Flying Corps. The idea of solitary aerial combat was much more attractive to him than fighting as one of a mass of unknown soldiers. After a crash, however, he had to give up flying and did, in fact, spend some time in the trenches of the Western Front, before being invalided home.

Intelligent, handsome, wounded young men of the upper classes were a godsend to the Conservative Party in the years just after the war and Mosley was soon offered a seat in Parliament (Harrow) which he won in the 1918 election. When he entered the House, he was, at twenty-two, the youngest member. Two years later he married Cimmie, the daughter of Lord Curzon, the Foreign Secretary. His future now seemed assured. He was clearly intelligent, he had a safe seat in Parliament and through his marriage he gained both money and good connections.

Yet Mosley could never settle. He was restless and soon discovered he had no real intellectual belief in conservatism. By 1924 he had become a member of the Labour Party. Many in the Party never accepted him. He and Cimmie still followed a luxurious lifestyle at a time of high unemployment and continuing poverty for the mass of British workers.

This hostility to Mosley was not entirely fair. During the twenties he thought deeply and with sincerity about the curse of unemployment. Almost alone, he developed a set of proposals for creating new jobs. He argued that the government should take a larger role in spending on public works and that British industry should be strongly protected against the competition of the outside world. These ideas were presented to the Labour Government of 1929 in which Mosley was a junior minister.

Sadly, they were rejected. The MacDonald government, battered by the economic crisis, seemed totally unable to consider fresh solutions to it. Mosley did not take defeat easily. He resigned his post and then took his plans both to the Labour MPs as a whole and to the Labour Party Conference of 1930. He defended his ideas with magnificent oratory. Both times, however, he was defeated, and he decided to leave the party.

Despite his defeat, Mosley had impressed many. Prominent figures of the left of the party, such as Nye Bevan, were attracted by his ideas. If Mosley had shown patience and remained in the Labour Party, a major political career might have awaited him.

However, Mosley lacked this patience and he felt betrayed. From now on he sought revenge on the traditional political parties he felt had rejected him. They had, he claimed, lost the will and vigour to govern. There was the need for a new political movement to replace the discredited old one. Mosley's first

13 Oswald Mosley takes a salute with Benito Mussolini, the leader of fascist Italy. Mussolini was to give Mosley both encouragement and money for British fascism.

attempt to set up an alternative, the so-called New Party, was a dismal failure. In the General Election of 1931 it received a total of only 36,000 votes.

It was now that Mosley drifted towards fascism. The first fascist leader, Mussolini, had now been in power for ten years and many were taken in by his exaggerated claims of Italian national revival. (Hitler, who was to show a much more brutal and racialist approach to fascism, was not yet in power.) Mosley visited Mussolini in 1932, was suitably impressed and was to receive his support, and, secretly, his money in the years that followed.

Many warned Mosley to keep clear of fascism. "In England anything on these lines is doomed to failure and ridicule," wrote Harold Nicolson, originally a supporter of Mosley. He was right. The British do not warm to foreign political ideas. Britain had never known the crisis of national identity and social disintegration that Italy and Germany had seen, and few believed in the need for a breakdown of the old system. It was already

clear to many that fascism implied racialism and violence in its pursuit of national greatness.

Mosley never wished to follow slavishly the German or Italian models of fascism. For him, at first, the main task was to restore economic independence to Britain, an independence which he believed was threatened by the forces of international capitalism centred in the City of London. He also promised that British fascism would avoid the darker sides of continental fascism.

The British Union of Fascists was founded in October 1932. Mosley called for those who would join him in "a great and hazardous adventure". In many ways, the movement was similar to those on the continent. There was a strong military atmosphere, with a uniform, a black shirt, marching, leaders and discipline. Publicity was built up by great mass meetings in which the ranks of Mosley's supporters would gather to hear him speak.

These similarities with its counterparts in Italy and Germany made British fascism immediately an object of suspicion to many. The growing and widely publicized brutality of Hitler's rule was bound to discredit Mosley.

14 The headquarters of the British Union of Fascists in Kings Road, Chelsea. There was a strong emphasis on military discipline. Notice the "guards".

15 A mass meeting of the British Union of Fascists. Mosley used many of the same techniques as the European fascist parties with "The Leader" isolated in front of his followers.

16 By 1936 Mosley's movement was failing. Increasingly, the movement tried to exploit anti-Jewish feeling. Here Mosley marches through the East End of London where he felt support might be strong.

17 In fact, the people of the East End organized a counter-demonstration which clashed with police in the "battle" of Cable Street, October 1936.

When, in June 1934, violence broke out at a fascist meeting at Olympia and stewards forcibly ejected those who interrupted Mosley's speech, the resulting publicity was enough to damn the movement.

Mosley was never to recover from this setback. His Union never appealed to more than a tiny minority of Britons. It put up no candidates in the 1935 General Election. The calibre of its members was low and continual internal bickering made matters worse. Despite Mosley's claim that his movement would avoid the excesses of continental fascism, anti-semitism had become a major element of British fascism by 1936. (It is only fair to add that, in contrast to what happened in Germany and Italy, not a single person lost their life in Britain as a result of fascist violence.)

In the later thirties, Mosley made no secret of his support for Germany, although he was not attracted by Hitler himself. In these years he did believe in rearming Britain to maintain the defence of the Empire. He saw no threat to the Empire, however, from the expansion of Germany into Eastern Europe and he did not support Britain's declaration of war in 1939. He and his second wife, Diana, were interned during the war, on account of their pro-German sympathies.

What was it in Mosley's personality that drove him into this troubled backwater of British politics? He had been a loner since childhood. Although he had been born into all the privileges of upper-class life, which he and his first wife, Cimmie, enjoyed to the full, he never felt at home there. He was clearly deeply hurt by his rejection by the Labour Party. More and more, he came to see himself as the lost leader, the one who had the vision to break through the decadent social and political life of Britain and create a new nation.

His sense of isolation was increased by the death of Cimmie in 1933. She was only thirty-four. Up to then, Mosley had diluted his political life with a flamboyant lifestyle, typical of that enjoyed by the upper classes of the period, with long holidays abroad, particularly in Venice, and weekends at large country houses.

Mosley was a compulsive womanizer, another sign of his restless and unsettled nature. Cimmie was caused increasing distress in the years before she died. At the time of her death, Mosley was already deeply involved with Diana Guinness who was to become his second wife. Nevertheless, the death of Cimmie must have been a major shock and after it, Mosley committed himself ever more vigorously to fascism. His social life became more limited and he thus cut himself off further from the mainstream of British life.

Harold Nicolson was right when he said that a fascist movement in Britain was doomed to ridicule. Much of the ridicule was bound to be attached to the leader. Mosley was certainly a fine orator and he was a fit and active man. He was not, however, superhuman, despite the efforts of some of his supporters to make him so.

Now he moves forward [wrote one of them] to a still greater destiny, an implacable figure looming ever more immense against the background of his times; through his own eager spirit so full of aspiration and boldness, symbolising the immortal spirit of his race. . . . Hail Mosley, patriot and revolutionary, leader of men.

It was an image impossible to sustain. In his biography of his father, Nicholas Mosley writes that Mosley got all dressed up as a fascist but somehow never had the ruthlessness to make himself a true fascist leader. His children quickly saw through the pretence. Nicholas Mosley writes of his sister, Vivien:

Viv, aged fourteen, was almost the only person who did not seem in awe of my father; she answered him back; often she even got in a bit of 'chaff' first. She would tell him how ridiculous he looked when, even for family photographs, he posed like Mussolini on the prow of his boat.

Any new political movement, let alone one which would inevitably be associated with the horrors of Nazi Germany, would have found it difficult to become established in the complacent political atmosphere of Britain in the 1930s. Mosley never seemed to realize just how alien fascism was to the British political tradition. He talked continually of a crisis which faced the nation, but somehow that crisis never seemed to erupt.

Mosley had withdrawn, in fact, into a political wilderness, and he remained isolated until his death in 1980. His biographer, Robert Skidelsky, has shown the strength and originality of his early ideas on unemployment. It was tragic that this undoubted originality could not have been used to stimulate mainstream political thought in the 1930s. The weakness in Mosley's character made him one of the most wasted men of his generation.

Nye Bevan (1897-1960)

Few among the mass of backbench MPs of the 1930s knew more about the effects of the Depression than Aneurin (Nye) Bevan, the tempestuous Labour member for Ebbw Vale, South Wales, and few were more ready to champion those who had suffered from it. Nye Bevan, born in the small mining town of Tredegar in 1897, had been a miner himself, entering the pits when only fourteen. He had seen the mining communities devastated by the slump in demand for coal in the 1920s and he himself had been unemployed.

Determined to dramatize the plight of the valleys, he entered the rough world of local Welsh politics and fought his way upwards, antagonizing many, enthralling others by his outspoken attacks on the coal-owners and their supporters. By 1929 he was selected as Labour candidate for Ebbw Vale and was victorious in the General Election of that year.

For many, Bevan remained no more than an unstable rebel, "a squalid nuisance", as Churchill was once to call him. All his life he hated institutions, uneasy even as a member of

18 Fernhill Colliery, South Wales. During a "stay-in" strike, in August 1936, relatives of the miners gather in sympathy.

19 Miners in the cage at the pithead of a South Wales mine. Note the lamps and working clothes.

the Labour Party. Even his closest friends were infuriated by his refusal to follow the conventional rules of politics. In his brilliant biography of Bevan, Michael Foot writes:

All the minutiae of politics bored him. His mind was formed in an entirely different mould and you could no more change it than persuade him to disown his working class ancestry. His eyes were fixed on the horizons of politics. He was obsessed by the broad, tumultuous movements in society and the world at large.

Even in his first Parliament, when still a junior and unknown member, he lost no time in attacking the giants. "Mr Bevan has no fear, he shrinks before no one," wrote one journalist, as he watched Bevan taking on two future Prime Ministers, Winston Churchill and Neville Chamberlain, and one great leader of the past, Bevan's fellow Welshman, David Lloyd George, savaged in a bitter attack.

Of course, this was not the whole story. Behind the rebellious facade, Bevan was a warm and caring man, a lover of humanity and always prepared to enjoy life to the full. Even his political opponents, bitterly attacked in public, could become close friends in private. A love for Wales remained central to him. As his wife, Jennie Lee, wrote:

It was the Duffryn Valley, the road over the Black Mountains, the lovely Welsh Hills quite close to Tredegar that meant most to him, then and always. From earliest boyhood they had added grace and spaciousness to his life. Always when we drove to Wales, as soon as the Welsh hills appeared in the distance, he began singing 'Home to our Mountains'.

In 1934 Bevan married Jennie Lee, another Labour member of the 1929 Parliament which was to prove so fateful for the Labour Party. Jennie lost her seat in the 1931 election. Like Bevan, she was passionately interested in the politics of the left, both at home and abroad, and it was some time before Nye could persuade her to marry him. The doubts were at last resolved and, as Michael Foot puts it, "two turbulent independent temperaments grew together into a union of utter trust and devotion".

The Bevans bought a cottage in Berkshire, Lane End Cottage, and here, among friends,

20 Nye Bevan and Jennie Lee after their marriage, 1934.

the true qualities of Nye's mind became apparent.

No one who was a frequent visitor to Lane End or their later establishments ever forgot the magic of those evenings. No one who was present at a session when he really talked ever forgot the experience. No one who knew him in those moods ever expected to meet anyone else who could spread the same enchantment by his gaiety, his originality, his laughter and his matchless powers of reasoning and argument. He was always probing, the brain was rarely inactive; the tongue was always searching for new phrases and formulations to awaken the imagination. . . . Out of the topics of the day he could spin a wonderful, delicate web of theory, a grand perspective on the forces shaping society; you went away from one of those evenings feeling rich, rich in the belief of what could be achieved if his creative intelligence and the ideas it generated could be given full rein. (Michael Foot)

These years were troubled and depressing ones for the Labour Party. Betrayed, as most members believed, by their leader Ramsay MacDonald in 1931 and then heavily defeated in the election of that year, the Party found it difficult to find a role. The leadership was always moderate, conscious perhaps that the only hope of political recovery lay in recapturing the support of the centre, ground held skilfully by Stanley Baldwin. Bevan was torn between his love and need for his Party and his scorn at the way he felt it failed to champion the real issues. "It is the whole spirit of leadership which is at fault," he wrote in July 1937.

It refuses to fight desperately and heroically in matters of key principles. It refuses to arouse the electorate on burning day to day issues such as the Means Test, the forty hour week, and Spain. . . . . It is too respectable and too statesmanlike, too frightened of offending the middle class.

Bevan was particularly scornful of the Party's failure to champion the unemployed. The most prominent organization in this field, the National Unemployed Workers' Movement, was, in fact, Communist-led and, as a result, was cold-shouldered by the Labour Party. Bevan found this unforgivable, and, defying the Labour leadership, he went on NUWM marches and spoke at their demonstrations.

In the Commons, itself, Bevan's greatest struggle was against the Unemployment Assistance Bill of 1934. This Bill attempted to standardize benefits, so that all unemployed

21 Bevan speaking. He was one of the most gifted speakers of the period, but dealt ruthlessly with his opponents.

would receive the same sum, whatever part of the country they came from. In many cases, however, the new national rate was lower than that paid by local authorities. To Bevan the Bill also brought more administrative barriers between the unemployed and the relief of their needs. "You want to suffocate the unemployed man's cries in a mass of bureaucracy," he thundered. Although the Bill became law, the outcry against it was such that it was two years before it was fully implemented.

The other major issue which consumed Bevan's energies in these years was the rising tide of fascism. For many, this was dramatized by the successful rebellion of the Spanish Army, helped by the fascist governments of Italy and Germany, against the Republican Government of Spain in 1936 – the Spanish Civil War. The Bevans had visited Spain before the war broke out and were immensely attracted by it. "He looked utterly at home in Andalusia," wrote Jennie of Nye. "He loved it. The vivid colouring, the smell and flavour of the place, the warmth, the dark, proud-spirited people."

Now Spain was being torn apart by war and the British government, supported at first by the Labour Party, had decided not to intervene. Bevan was furious. If the left (the Republican Government and its supporters) were defeated in Spain, the left everywhere would suffer:

What is going to be the effect upon the vitality of socialism throughout the world if our comrades in Spain are slaughtered and democracy is on its back as a consequence of our acquiescence in neutrality?

Bevan's pleas were not successful. Some help was given by the left in Britain to the Republican cause, and many went to fight, but it was not enough to prevent the victory of the Nationalist forces.

It is not surprising, therefore, that Bevan became increasingly disillusioned with his party in the late 1930s. He became convinced that the only way forward was to establish a movement of all the parties of the left to

22 A march of the NUWM in 1932 against the detested Means Test. Bevan defied Labour Party leaders to give support to this Communist-led organization.

struggle more effectively for socialism and to face up to the forces of fascism. Thus he joined Stafford Cripps, a brilliant left-wing intellectual, to build up a Popular Front of left-wing parties. This was too much for the Labour Party and Cripps and Bevan were expelled.

Bevan knew, however, that his only real home lay with the Labour Party. As he had told Jennie Lee many years earlier,

It is the Labour Party or nothing. I know all its faults, all its dangers. But it is the Party that we have taught millions of working people to look to and to regard as their own.

He was readmitted in December 1939.

Bevan was only forty-two in 1939 and many of his greatest achievements lay ahead. He led a long battle against what he considered the dictatorship of Churchill in the Second World War. In the triumphant Labour Government of 1945-50, he was to play a major role as architect of the National Health Service and as an important founder of the modern Welfare State. He died in 1960.

Neville Chamberlain (1869-1940)

When, on 3 September 1939, Neville Chamberlain, Prime Minister of Britain, broadcast to the nation the news that Britain was at war, he expressed his despair as follows:

You can imagine what a bitter blow it is to me that all my long struggle to win peace has failed. Yet I cannot believe that there is anything more or anything different that I could have done or that would have been more successful.

Only a year before, many would have agreed. On his return from making the Munich Agreement with Hitler in September 1938, Chamberlain had, indeed, been hailed as a hero, the man who had brought peace through negotiation. Now it could be seen how he had been outwitted and exploited by Hitler. All his hopes had been dashed.

Neville Chamberlain came from a celebrated political family which had built its power base in Birmingham. His father, Joseph Chamberlain, was one of the most brilliant and outspoken politicians of the late nineteenth century and had worked his way up to the post of Colonial Secretary in Lord Salisbury's government of 1895-1902. Joseph Chamberlain married three times. By his first marriage he had a son, Austen, onto whom all his political ambitions were transferred and Austen was, indeed, to rise as high as his father had done, becoming Foreign Secretary in Baldwin's government of 1924-9. Neville, the son of a second marriage, was born in 1869.

Neville Chamberlain's mother died on the eve of his sixth birthday and, since his father was absorbed in national affairs, Neville was a neglected child and was particularly unhappy at school. He was destined to go into the family business and in 1890, when he was still only twenty-one, his father sent him to manage a sisal estate he had bought in the West Indies. The business was a failure.

Chamberlain spent five years in almost total isolation, trying to make the unsuitable crop take root. Just at an age when he most needed confidence and human company to overcome his shyness, Chamberlain was deprived of both.

Back in Britain, Chamberlain continued in the family business and then followed the family tradition of local politics in Birmingham. He was Lord Mayor of the City in 1915 and was already acquiring a reputation as a good administrator. He always appeared, however, as a remote figure and it was only to his close family (he married when he was forty-two) that a more human side of him emerged. He loved music and, when he later took up shooting, found a real love of the countryside.

In 1918, now nearly fifty, Chamberlain was returned as a Conservative member of Parliament for Birmingham. His abilities were soon recognized and he was made Minister of Health in Baldwin's government of 1924-9. This was a post which suited both his talents and his temperament. He brought to the post, one journalist wrote,

much knowledge of local government, a deep if rather nineteenth century passion for social reform, inherited from his father, a formidable memory for detail and a talent for close administration that won him the justified respect of his officials.

In the National Government of 1931 he was a natural choice for Chancellor of the Exchequer. Here again he showed the same qualities, a careful, if unimaginative, management of the nation's money. He presided over the steady return to prosperity, even if his policies did little to hasten it. "Of the senior ministers of this Government," writes Robert Rhodes James in *The British Revolution*, only Neville Chamberlain enhanced his reputation, his massive competence and self-assurance evoking respect but little affection.

When Baldwin retired as Prime Minister in 1937, there was no other acceptable successor. At the age of sixty-eight, Chamberlain was Prime Minister.

Once he was in his new post, Chamberlain's natural reserve caused him to distance himself from his colleagues. As Robert Rhodes James puts it:

By March 1938, Chamberlain had established a congenial, subservient and mediocre government which he personally dominated, usually ignored and, as some thought, bullied . . . his mastery of the House of Commons and Cabinet was complete. His weapons were immense application, mastery of his subject and a freezing belligerence which his opponents found profoundly intimidating.

23 Neville Chamberlain meets with Adolf Hitler, September 1938. To Chamberlain, Hitler was "a reasonable man" with whom lasting agreement could be reached.

The dominant concern of the day was bound to be foreign affairs. It was a field in which Chamberlain had little experience and for which he showed little inclination. "Chamberlain has no conception really of world politics. Nor does he welcome advice from those who have," wrote Harold Nicolson, the writer and MP, whose own speciality was foreign affairs. There was, however, an urgent need to define a clear policy of how to deal with Hitler, now firmly in control of Germany and engaged in a heavy rearmament programme.

Chamberlain failed to recognize the true nature of Nazism. His weakness in this respect was well summed up by Duff Cooper, a junior minister in the first months of Chamberlain's government:

He [Chamberlain] had never moved in the great world of politics or finance, and the continent of Europe was a closed book. He had been a successful Lord Mayor of Birmingham and for him the Dictators of Germany and Italy were like the Lord Mayors of Liverpool and Manchester, who might belong to different political parties and have different interests, but who must desire the welfare of humanity and be fundamentally reasonable, decent men like himself. This profound misconception lay at the root of his policy and explains his mistakes.

Chamberlain believed, as did many others, that Hitler and the Nazis had a few specified grievances, rooted in the way Germany had been treated at the end of the First World War. Once these grievances had been settled, preferably by negotiation, then Germany would be satisfied and the brutalities of the regime and the aggressive talk of expansion would fade.

The emphasis, then, was on negotiation and there were many reasons why this seemed the most sensible way forward. Many were haunted by memories of how the First World War had started, by reckless confrontation between the nations of Europe. Sitting round a table discussing differences seemed infinitely preferable. A policy of confrontation with Germany involved the risk of war, and thus the need for rearmament. Could Britain afford this when her domestic needs were so great? All decent men put welfare before guns. Even if Britain did confront Germany, it looked as if she would be alone. France did not appear to be a trustworthy ally. The United States had isolated herself completely from European affairs. There remained a profound distrust of Russia, especially now that Stalin had purged the Russian army so effectively of its leading generals.

All the pressures, therefore, were in favour of the policy of appeasement, the settlement of differences by negotiation. Such a policy might well have worked if Hitler had been reasonable, with limited ambitions and ready to keep agreements. His ambitions were, however, enormous and they became even more so every time he was given concessions. Nazism had acquired a momentum of its own and it was a sad fact that only confrontation would quell it.

Chamberlain brought a sense of urgency to the policy of appeasement. It was almost as if he felt that his own life was coming to an end and he had a personal mission to bring about peace before it was too late. As he told the House of Commons in 1938,

It is to such tasks – the winning back of confidence, the gradual removal of hostility between nations until they feel that they can safely discard their weapons, one by one, that I would wish to devote what energy and time may be left to me before I hand over my office to younger men.

Hitler was to give him his chance. It had always been one of Hitler's declared aims to reunite the German people who lived outside Germany with their fatherland. Britain and France had, in fact, accepted this right of self-determination for nationalities at the Versailles Settlement after the First World War. Germany had been excluded and had been forbidden to unite with the German peoples of Austria. In 1938, however, Hitler incorporated Austria into Germany. Britain offered no protest. Hitler's next request was for the incorporation of those Germans living in the western borderlands of Czechoslovakia, the so-called Sudeten Germans. However, if he took this territory, he would be depriving Czechoslovakia of the strategic mountain ranges which protected her from Germany. Such a handover could only be justified if Czechoslovakia agreed to it and Hitler could really be trusted not to move further east into non-German parts of Czechoslovakia.

The Czechs sensed the danger and resisted Hitler's claims. They hoped that the nations of western Europe would support them. For Chamberlain, however, the desire to agree with Hitler was so great that he disregarded the fears of Czechoslovakia. When Hitler threatened war if he could not get his way, Chamberlain told the British public who were beginning to prepare for the possible conflict,

How horrible, fantastic, incredible it is that we should be digging trenches here because of a quarrel in a far-away country between people of whom we know nothing.

No phrase could sum up more vividly the insularity of Chamberlain's approach to world affairs. The Czechs were bullied into acceptance of Hitler's terms and Chamberlain, with the support of the French Government, signed over the Sudeten Germans to Hitler.

24 March 1939. The Nazi wolves gobble up Czechoslovakia. Chamberlain offers help only when it is too late. A cartoon by Low, a determined opponent of the appeasement policy.

"Excuse me, but did you hear a piercing scream?"

25 September 1939. A shattered Chamberlain, his plans for peace in ruins, tells the nation that Britain is at war with Germany.

Chamberlain flew home from this so-called Munich Agreement in triumph. As he stepped from his plane, he held up a piece of paper which he and Hitler had signed, expressing their desire that their two countries need never go to war again. He had written earlier of Hitler: "I got the impression that here was a man who could be relied on when he had given his word."

Chamberlain's triumph was to be shortlived. In March 1939 Hitler moved his troops into the now unprotected Czechoslovakia. It was now suddenly clear how far Chamberlain had been misled. Hastily, the British and French reversed their policy. They guaranteed the borders of other nations of Eastern Europe. Hitler refused to believe that they would, in fact, fight. He went ahead with his plans for the conquest of Poland.

When he struck in September 1939, there was, indeed, hesitation from both Chamberlain and the French. This time, however, the mood in Britain had changed. Chamberlain was forced to declare war.

Chamberlain lasted as Prime Minister until May 1940. He did not lead the country with energy or enthusiasm and his own party, at length, revolted against him. Churchill took his place as Prime Minister. Within a few months Chamberlain was dead.

26 Another cartoon by Low. The Nazi tiger has now eaten up Chamberlain, leaving only his umbrella, top hat and moustache.

The End

Winston Churchill (1874-1965)

A man larger than life, composed of bigger and simpler elements than ordinary men, a gigantic historical figure during his own lifetime, superhumanly bold, strong and imaginative, an orator of prodigious powers, the saviour of his country, a mythical hero who belongs to legend as much as to reality, the largest human being of our time.

So wrote Isaiah Berlin in his assessment of Winston Churchill. He was, of course, writing after the Second World War when Churchill's

27 Winston Churchill in relaxed mood. This photograph, taken around 1930, shows Churchill enjoying a favourite hobby, bricklaying.

enormous talents had at last been matched with a cause worthy of them, the leadership of an embattled Britain during her struggle with Nazi Germany. Nevertheless, even before the war, Churchill was a figure of world renown.

By 1930 Churchill had already been a Member of Parliament for thirty years. Among the Cabinet posts he had held had been Home Secretary in a pre-war Liberal government, First Lord of the Admiralty in the First World War and Chancellor of the Exchequer in Baldwin's government of 1924-9. He was already celebrated as a writer, having completed a biography of his father, the Conservative politician, Lord Randolph

Churchill, a five-volume history of the First World War and an account of his early restless life in parts of the British Empire. He was about to embark on a four-volume biography of his ancestor, the first Duke of Marlborough. By the late 1930s he was to be earning over £200,000 a year (in 1980 prices) from his writings.

However, despite these achievements, Churchill was regarded with suspicion in many circles. It was difficult to know where his true political loyalties lay. He had started life as a Conservative, then joined the Liberals and later, in the early 1920s, rejoined the Conservatives. Many felt that his naval plans, when at the Admiralty in the First War, had been unnecessarily reckless, that he was tempted too easily by the glamour of battle. His vivid and romantic view of history was coloured by cavalry charges and conquest and seemed far from the more peace-loving spirit of the thirties. Stanley Baldwin summed up the general opinion as follows:

When Winston was born lots of fairies swooped down on his cradle gifts – imagination, eloquence, industry, ability, and then came a fairy who said 'No one person has a right to so many gifts', picked him up and gave him such a shake and twist that with all these gifts he was denied judgement and wisdom. And that is why while we delight to listen to him in this House we do not take his advice.

By the 1930s Churchill had fallen out with his party on the question of India. He had spent three of his early years there and had a rather romantic picture of the British-in-India living out their imperial mission to the end of time. He felt that the Government of India Bill was an unjustified and unnecessary surrender of British rule. Few Conservatives supported him and despite a brilliant and sustained campaign against the Bill, Churchill seemed only to confirm the views of those who felt he was lacking in judgement.

Further confirmation came during the Abdication Crisis of 1936. Churchill was a fervent, if, again, rather romantic supporter of the King. When the crisis reached its height in December, Churchill pleaded that the King be given more time to come to a decision about his future with Mrs Simpson. However, the feeling of the House of Commons was that the matter should be resolved immediately and when Churchill rose to state his case on 7 December, he was howled down in what one observer described as "one of the angriest manifestations I have ever heard directed against any man in the House of Commons".

When Churchill launched his greatest campaign of all, about the need to rearm in face of the rising might of Nazi Germany, it was as an isolated and mistrusted figure, with a reputation as a warmonger. He seemed to be battling against the spirit of the age and it is not surprising that he was not listened to.

Churchill's recognition of the dangers to Britain of a revived Germany dated from as early as 1930. In November 1932, when there

28 Members of the Hitler Youth movement. Churchill felt they would never be content with just marching, but would search for military glory.

was some discussion as to whether Germany should be allowed equal status in armaments, Churchill warned:

Equal status is not what Germany is seeking. All those bands of sturdy Teutonic youths, marching through the streets and roads of Germany, with the light of desire in their eyes to suffer for their fatherland, are not looking for status. They are looking for weapons, and when they have the weapons, believe me they will then ask for the return of lost territories and lost colonies. . . .

This was even before Hitler had come to power. As Nazi control of Germany was consolidated and German rearmament began, Churchill warned ever more insistently of the danger ahead, both to Europe and to Britain.

Why did Churchill, almost alone, see the threat from a revived Germany so early and clearly? Part of the answer lies, perhaps, in his view of history. Few politicians have had such a strong sense of the past. For Churchill, European history was a story of ambition and conquest. He, himself, was absorbed for much of the decade in the study of the military campaigns of the Duke of Marlborough. He did not believe that things had changed, even after the devastating shock of the First World War. The search for power and domination continued and it was not surprising to Churchill that a nation with the potential military and economic power of Germany should seek revenge for her defeat in the First World War. He was ready for the first signs of her revived ambitions.

What should Britain's response be? For four hundred years, Churchill argued, it had been her policy not to let one nation dominate Europe. Thus Britain must be rearmed and prepared to confront German aggression. Of course, this could not be done alone and, as in the past, alliances should be made. As Churchill wrote in 1936,

I would marshal all the countries including Soviet Russia from the Baltic southward round to the Belgian coast, all agreeing to stand by any victim of unprovoked aggression. I would put combined pressure upon every country neighbouring to Germany to subscribe to this and guarantee an armed force for the purpose.

Churchill's campaign for rearmament centred on the need for air power. It was a common belief in the thirties, and one Churchill shared, that the next war would be won or lost in the air, or rather by the devastation of mass bombing. The power of the bomber was wildly exaggerated, with alarming predictions of the casualties bombing would cause. In 1934 Churchill himself claimed that a few days of German bombing would kill or maim thirty to forty thousand Londoners and drive three or four million out into the open countryside. In 1937 the Cabinet was presented with estimates of some 600,000 British killed and 1,200,000 wounded in the first sixty days of a war with Germany. (The actual figures for five and a half years of warfare were 60,000 dead and 240,000 wounded.)

Defence debates of the thirties thus concentrated overwhelmingly on air forces and, in fact, became obsessed with numbers.

How many front line bombers did the German Luftwaffe have now and how many would it have by 1939? What would be the equivalent British figures? Churchill argued that Britain was falling behind. We now know that the estimates of the strength of the German Luftwaffe were exaggerated and that Britain by 1939 was producing more planes than the Germans were. The debates over *numbers* also obscured the vital issue. How were the planes to be used? Churchill argued for fighters to defend and bombers (aiming at military targets) for attack. He continued to believe right up to 1940 that the air force *alone* could win the war.

Just as he overemphasized the importance of the air force, so Churchill underestimated the importance of the army. In 1938 he said, "One thing is certain about the next war, namely that the armies will use their spades more often than they use their bayonets." He failed to recognize the way that tanks could be used to spearhead attacks and how air-power could be used, not alone, but in conjunction with armies to break through the enemy lines. In fact, it was cuts in arms expenditure that Churchill made when he was Chancellor of the Exchequer in the 1920s which had led to the British tank programme being downgraded. Churchill himself preferred cavalry and was sad to let it go.

Thus, while Churchill was certainly right in his immediate recognition of the dangers of

29 After a slow start, Britain was by 1939 rearming fast. One of the first squadrons of Spitfires is paraded at Duxford airfield.

Nazi Germany, he did not necessarily choose the right response. It was German military might backed by air-power which was to dominate Europe and in retaliation it was overwhelmingly American and Russian military might which was to destroy it.

As Britain embarked on her policy of appeasement, Churchill spoke ever more eloquently of the dangers of coming to terms with Germany. For instance, when the British Government failed to make any response to the incorporation of Austria into Germany in March 1938, Churchill warned of the downward path to darkness that Britain was following:

For five years I have talked to the House [of Commons] on these matters, not with very great success. I have watched this famous island descending incontinently, fecklessly, the stairway which leads to a dark gulf. It is a fine broad stairway at the beginning, but after a bit the carpet ends. A little farther on there are only flagstones, and a little farther on still these break beneath your feet. . . .

It was moving, evocative language like this which was one of Churchill's major gifts and which, in the Second World War, was to be the force which inspired the nation. Even those who disagreed with him would pack in to the House of Commons to hear Churchill speak, and again and again he would catch an atmosphere with his words. When the Munich Agreement was made in September 1938, Churchill spoke of the fate of Czechoslovakia: "All is over, silent, mournful, abandoned, broken, Czechoslovakia recedes into the darkness." In the same speech, he talked of the folly of trying to negotiate with Germany:

There never can be friendship between the British democracy and the Nazi power, that power which spurns Christian ethics, which cheers its onward course by a barbarous paganism, which vaunts the spirit of aggression and conquest, which derives strength and perverted pleasure from persecution, and uses, as we have seen, with pitiless brutality the threat of murderous force. That Power cannot ever be the trusted friend of the British democracy.

A few months after these words, Churchill's warnings were shown to be justified. In March 1939, the rest of Czechoslovakia was incorporated into Germany and Hitler began to plan for the conquest of Poland. When the attack came in September 1939, Britain went to war in Poland's defence.

Churchill spoke in the House of Commons:

This is not a question of fighting for Danzig or fighting for Poland. We are fighting to save the whole world from the pestilence of Nazi tyranny and in defence of all that is most sacred in man. This is no war of domination or imperial aggrandisement or material gain; no war to shut any country out of its sunlight and means of progress. It is a war, viewed in its inherent quality, to establish, on impregnable rocks, the rights of the individual, and it is a war to establish and revive the stature of man. . . .

Now that war had come, it was felt that Churchill must have a big share in conducting it. He was made First Lord of the Admiralty, the post he had held in the First World War. In May 1940, following the resignation of Chamberlain, he became Prime Minister and remained as Britain's leader during the war years, seeing her eventually victorious.

WRITERS

As the stormclouds gathered on the continent in the 1930s, British writers had to decide on their own response to events. What was the duty of the writer? Could he or she ignore what was going on and continue to write, for instance, novels on the lives and preoccupations of ordinary people? Was there not a duty, at the very least, to observe and describe what was going on, so that the public could be better informed and warned? Or should the writer come down off a pedestal and become actively involved in politics – even taking up arms if necessary?

For the Communist poet, John Cornford, active commitment was the only true role. Writing was just one part of a life lived totally for political ideals. In his poem *Full Moon at Tierz, Before the Storming of Huesca*, Cornford describes his feelings as he waits in the moonlight for the start of a battle of the Spanish Civil War. The struggle for freedom in Spain is part of the indivisible worldwide struggle for freedom.

England is silent under the same moon,
From the Clydeside to the gutted pits of Wales
The innocent mask conceals that soon
Here, too, our freedom's swaying in the scales.
O understand before too late
Freedom was never won without a fight.

The most sustained effort to involve writers in the struggle for "freedom" came from the Left Book Club, founded by the socialist publisher, Victor Gollancz. Members of the Club were circulated with the Club's choice of relevant books. "The aim of the Club is a simple one," it was stated in 1937:

It is to help in the terribly urgent struggle for world peace and a better social and economic order and against Fascism, by giving (to all those who are determined to play their part in the struggle) such knowledge as will immensely increase their efficiency.

The Club was an immediate success. By 1937 it had 50,000 members and had circulated nearly a million books. Members met in local groups to discuss the latest publications. For those of the left who felt isolated and vulnerable after the continuing successes of fascism, it was a vital rallying-point. All in all, the Club was a remarkable attempt to use literature to create commitment.

The three writers described in this chapter made their commitment in different ways. For Virginia Woolf, writing was very much a private activity. Her novels were about private lives and the intimate problems of relationships between human beings. These relationships were, it is true, carried out against a backdrop of events, but these events seldom dominate or disturb the pattern of life. In fact, in order to write, Virginia Woolf needed to be sheltered from outside reality, and she did her best to avoid being involved in active politics.

W.H. Auden was of a different and younger generation. Although not originally interested in politics, he found that he could not stand aside. His poems describe the decay of society and the threat of dictatorship. Auden did go to Spain, as an observer, and he sided himself with the struggle against fascism. Yet, he never had much faith in the alternatives offered by the left and by 1939 had come to feel that poetry could achieve little. He left Europe for exile in the United States.

The most committed and politically active of the three was George Orwell. He observed the life of the poor by becoming a tramp himself and by visiting decaying towns such as Wigan. His *Road to Wigan Pier* was, in fact, a Left Book Club choice, one of the few still read today. In the Spanish Civil War, he actually fought and was wounded. To this extent, Orwell took his commitment further than Auden did.

These writers did not change history. Auden and Orwell are both probably better-known today than they were in the thirties and much of their best work was still to come. Public events and the actions of politicians overshadowed them and drowned their voices. Nevertheless, they have much to tell us about this decade.

Virginia Woolf (1882-1941)

She was extremely beautiful, with an austere intellectual beauty of bone and outline, with large melancholy eyes under carved lids, and the nose and the lips, the long cheekbones of a Gothic Madonna. Her voice, light, musical, with a throaty note to it, was one of her great charms. She was tall and thin and her hands were exquisite. She used to spread them out to the fire and they were so transparent one fancied one saw the long fragile bones through the skin.

So wrote Rosamund Lehmann, one of Virginia Woolf's admirers. For those who met her, Virginia Woolf was one of the most fascinating women of her generation. She had an acutely sensitive awareness of the world around her, which was immensely attractive, and her letters and diaries sparkle with her observations. To the general public, her greatest fame was as a novelist, a fame assured by the early 1930s. She was also deeply concerned with the struggles of educated women in a male-dominated world.

Virginia Woolf was born in 1882. Her father, Leslie Stephen, was one of the great Victorian intellectuals. He had married Virginia's mother as his second wife and there were four children of the marriage, Thoby and Adrian, Virginia and Vanessa, the sister who was always to remain closest to Virginia. The children grew up "in an atmosphere always charged with ideas and intelligent conversation frequently generated by the presence of England's leading intellectuals and the resources of a great library" (Michael Rosenthal, *Virginia Woolf*). It was an atmosphere which was to set a pattern for the rest of Virginia Woolf's life. Always shy, she was only really at home among a small circle of intellectual friends.

Tragically, Virginia's mother died when she was only thirteen and her father fell into despair and decline. It added to the deep-rooted sense of isolation which was to last throughout her life. When her father died in 1904, Virginia suffered a mental breakdown

30 Virginia Woolf in 1931.

and there was further tragedy when her brother, Thoby, died of typhoid in 1906. Virginia never entirely recovered from these blows and was to remain always vulnerable to mental collapse. The love of her friends and the approval of her work by literary critics were to be essential for her good health.

Her greatest support came from her husband, Leonard Woolf, whom she married in 1912. Woolf had just returned from Ceylon where he had been six years in the British colonial administration. He had now resigned and was to devote his life to political journalism. He probably did not realize how fragile his wife was until, in 1913, she suffered another major mental breakdown which was to leave her ill for over two years. She became increasingly dependent on his care and continued support.

Virginia Woolf first achieved success as a novelist in the 1920s with *Mrs Dalloway* and *To the Lighthouse*. In addition, she wrote a vast amount of literary criticism and she and Leonard founded and ran a printing press, the Hogarth Press, which printed their own books and those of their friends.

The Woolfs remained based in London, usually in Bloomsbury. Around them a circle of friends, the so-called Bloomsbury Group, had grown up. The group was founded in the early 1900s from among Thoby's Cambridge friends and was to continue right up to the 1930s. Its members shared a common belief in the importance of personal friendship and the creative arts. It was a group celebrated by many as one of the real centres of English intellectual life, envied and criticized by others as a snobbish and isolated elite. For Virginia Woolf, however, this circle of friends provided a desperately needed security.

The Woolfs also had a country home, Monk's House in Rodmell, Sussex, and the peace here was essential to Virginia as a contrast to her busy social life in London. As she wrote in June 1932,

Back from a good week end at Rodmell – a week end of no talking, sinking at once into deep safe book reading; and then sleep: clear transparent; with the may tree like a breaking wave outside;

and all the garden green tunnels, mounds of green: and then to wake into the hot still day, and never a person to be seen, never an interruption: the place to ourselves: the long hours.

For many who met her, Virginia Woolf appeared vivacious, lively, full of laughter, but it was often a mask. "Oh, I'm so tired," she wrote in July 1932,

I sometimes think people cannot know what they do to me when they ask me to 'see' them: how they hold me in the scorching light: how I dry and shrivel: how I lie awake at night longing for rest.

Virginia Woolf's perceptions of the world around her can be found in her two major novels of the 1930s, *The Waves* (1931) and *The Years* (1937). The characters in both come from the same background, middle-class, with some private money, a childhood in Victorian England. In *The Waves* there are six central characters, each with a different outlook on life, and through them Virginia Woolf examines a variety of responses to the problems of living. In *The Years* it is the Pargiter family whose lives are described as they unfold over fifty years. Virginia Woolf's characters have a sense of isolation, they never really come to understand the world around them and they wonder why they appear in some way to have failed as human beings. Nothing in life, above all relationships, seems to provide any real fulfilment. "We cannot help each other – we are all deformed," says North, one of the characters in *The Years*. Behind the scenes, there are landmarks, the waves and the sea, the ceaseless bustle of London traffic, but the characters do not understand what this continuity can offer them. The richness and sensitivity of Virginia Woolf's writing make up for the lack of events, for the sense of drift and the emptiness of life which is a prominent theme in her work.

The outside world does not often intrude into the lives of these characters and they are only dimly aware of the sinister developments of the decade. In *The Years*, one character, Peggy, does begin to realize how fragile their way of life has become. In the midst of a party, she stops to listen.

Far away she heard the sounds of the London night; a horn hooted; a siren wailed on the river. The far-away sounds, the suggestion they brought in of other worlds, indifferent to this world, of people toiling, grinding, in the heart of darkness, in the depths of night, made her say over Eleanor's words, Happy in this world, happy with living people. But how can one be happy? she asked herself in a world bursting with misery. On every placard at every street corner was Death; or worse – tyranny; brutality; torture; the fall of civilization; the end of freedom. We here, she thought, are only sheltering under a leaf, which will be destroyed.

Virginia Woolf's novels are, perhaps, too caught up in the preoccupations of her own personal dilemmas to give us a genuine picture of the 1930s. Even the class she describes was a disappearing one. She did, however, take a more public stance with her works on the position of women, *A Room of One's Own* (1929) and *Three Guineas* (1938). The first is a gently stated study of how women are denied the possibility of developing their personalities and creative powers in a male-dominated world. They must, she argues, be given space, a room of their own, and independence, five hundred pounds a year. In

31 Virginia Woolf asked that a woman be given £500 a year and a room of her own in order to be able to write. Life for the ordinary working woman fell far short of these ideals. Here women work in a shirt factory.

32 Women working in the fields in Kent, 1933. Agriculture was as depressed as industry in the early 1930s. Note the horse-drawn plough.

Three Guineas, written ten years later, the argument is more forceful and reflects a growing bitterness that Virginia Woolf felt not only about men but about the mounting violence in Europe, which she saw as the natural result of male dominance. Her solution that peace would follow when women were given a position of equality in society appears inadequate in face of the tumultuous events that were already shaking Europe. Nevertheless, these two works have provided Virginia Woolf with a lasting influence on feminist thought.

On a wider front, Virginia Woolf was not much interested in politics. In 1930 she described her memories of a meeting of a Women's Cooperative Guild:

All those questions, I found myself thinking, which matter so intensely to the people here, questions of sanitation and education and wages, this demand for an extra shilling, or another year at school, for eight hours instead of nine behind a counter or in a mine, leave me, in my blood and bones, untouched.

In his biography of Virginia Woolf, her nephew Quentin Bell records his own exasperation with her failure to become more involved in politics:

I recall her during these years [the mid-thirties]

at the meetings of the Rodmell Labour Party, a small group of which she was, for a time, the Secretary, and I remember my despair, when I was trying to get the party to pass resolutions urging the formation of a United Front — or something equally urgent, vital and important — and Virginia managed to turn the debate in such a way that it developed into an exchange of Rodmell gossip. In this of course she was much nearer the feelings of the masses, if one may thus describe the six or seven members of the Rodmell Labour Party, than I was. I wanted to talk politics, the masses wanted to talk about the vicar's wife.

The thirties, however, brought the great political questions into everyone's home. No one was immune from bombing or the threat of foreign conquest. This reality came home to Virginia Woolf when her nephew, Julian Bell, was killed in Spain in 1937. She was appalled. "Julian's death seems the most complete waste you can imagine," she wrote to a friend, and later,

What made him do it? I suppose it is a fever in the blood of the younger generation we cannot possibly understand. I have never known anyone of my generation have that feeling about a war.

Virginia Woolf was, of course, strongly anti-fascist. Everything in fascism was a direct threat to the way of life she valued so much. Yet she could never bring herself to understand the commitment of those who were prepared to use violence against it.

When war did break out in 1939, the Woolfs did not feel part of it. The struggle still seemed to concern others, not themselves. As Hitler's armies moved into Western Europe, they agreed that they might commit suicide together if things got worse. In 1940 their London house was bombed. In March 1941, Virginia, alone at Rodmell, felt overwhelmed by another mental collapse. This time she did not have the strength to fight it. On 28 March she went down to the river, filled her pockets with stones and drowned herself.

W.H. Auden (1907-73)

The 1930s were an age of anxiety and few could capture this mood as well as the poet W.H. Auden. In his early poems he describes the decaying society he sees around him during the Depression, the empty factories and the silent machinery. The old ruling classes of England have had their day and it is as if society is in transition, waiting for a new phase of history to begin. For Auden, however, unlike more politically committed members of his generation, there was little hope for the future. He saw the old world being replaced by one of tension and insecurity, of dictatorial leadership, not by a workers' paradise. After visiting Spain and seeing at first hand the bitterness of the Civil War, Auden felt there was little the poet could achieve in Europe and in 1939 he left for the United States.

Auden was born in 1907, the youngest of three brothers. His father was a doctor, taking up a post as Birmingham's Medical Officer of Health soon after Auden was born. It was an affectionate, intellectual family in which Auden, as the youngest, seems to have been somewhat spoiled by his mother. He developed a vivid imagination and by the age of fifteen had decided that he wished to be a poet. By the time he reached Christ Church, Oxford in 1925 he was already much more widely read and intellectually aware than his fellow students. He had a confidence in his vocation as a poet which overawed many who were not so sure of their futures and he soon set himself up as a sort of father figure, helping other young poets who came to him for advice. "Calling on Auden was a serious business," recalled Stephen Spender, another leading poet of the thirties. "One made an appointment." Spender found that Auden approved only six lines of his poetry in as many weeks.

Auden developed an eccentric lifestyle at Oxford. He drew his curtains during the day and worked by artificial light, he ate voraciously and he slept under an enormous pile of bedclothes, even apparently adding a carpet or curtains if he felt like it. He was homosexual and remained so all his life.

After leaving Oxford, Auden spent some time in Berlin, in the years before the Nazis came to power a centre of cultural and sexual freedom. When he returned to Britain, he settled as a teacher, first at a run-down private school near Glasgow, Larchfield Academy, and then at a more successful school, Downs School, near the Malvern Hills. In 1935 he spent a few months working with the Post Office's Documentary Film Unit where his best-known contribution was a verse commentary for the film *Night Mail*.

All these years Auden was writing and his range of literary output was enormous – poetry, of course, plays, travel books, book reviews. By 1935 he felt he could support himself by his writing and in the later thirties he spent much time travelling, to Iceland, to Spain to observe the Civil War and to China, again to observe a war, between China and Japan.

Like so many of his generation, Auden saw around him a Britain in decay. In a poem of 1930 he wrote as follows:

Get there if you can and see the land you once
    were proud to own
Though the roads have almost vanished and the
    expresses never run:
Smokeless chimneys, damaged bridges,
    rotting wharves and choked canals,
Tramlines buckled, smashed trucks lying on
    their sides across the rails;
Power-stations locked, deserted, since they
    drew the boiler fires;
Pylons fallen or subsiding, trailing dead high-
    tension wires;
Head-gears gaunt on grass-grown pit-banks,
    seams abandoned years ago;
Drop a stone and listen for its splash in flooded
    dark below.

33 Industrial decay – a steel factory reduced to ruins.

It was not only the physical structure of Britain that was in decay, it was the people themselves. Auden surveys the old ruling classes:

As for our upper class:
Let's be frank a moment, fellows — they won't pass
Mayors, Vicars, Lawyers, Doctors, Advertisers, Maiden Aunts
They're all in a funk but they daren't do a bunk,
Either rufflers or mousers they haven't a chance.
(*The Orators*, 1931)

If society is dying, what will take its place? For many on the left, the collapse of industrial, capitalist society had been long predicted. They had visions of what would replace it, some form of socialism. For Auden there was no such hope — he saw a world of tension and anxiety. "Have things gone too far already?" he wrote in 1930,

Are we done for? Must we wait
Heavy doom's approaching footsteps regular down miles of straight;
Run the whole night through in gumboots, stumble on and gasp for breath,
Terrors drawing close and closer, winter landscape, fox's death.

The image of being hunted by "doom's approaching footsteps" is common in Auden. It is perhaps most vigorously expressed in another poem, written in 1932, *O, What is that Sound?* Here a man and a woman are standing by their home, watching soldiers manoeuvring in the valley below. Suddenly, the soldiers seems to be leaving the valley and coming towards the onlookers . . .

O why have they left the road down there;
Why are they suddenly wheeling, wheeling?
Perhaps a change in their orders, dear;
Why are you kneeling?

O haven't they stopped for the doctor's care;
Haven't they reined their horses, their horses?
Why, they are none of them wounded, dear,
None of these forces.

O is it the parson they want with white hair;
Is it the parson, is it, is it?
No, they are passing his gateway, dear,
Without a visit.

O it must be the farmer who lives so near;
It must be the farmer so cunning, so cunning?
They have passed the farm already, dear,
And now they are running.

O, where are you going? Stay with me here!
Were the vows you swore me, deceiving, deceiving?
No, I promised to love you, dear,
But I must be leaving.

O it's broken the lock and splintered the door,
O it's the gate where they are turning, turning:
Their feet are heavy on the floor
And their eyes are burning.

The soldiers have picked their victims and come to claim them.

In Auden's opinion, one of the most likely developments in the future would be the rise of a dictatorship. Certainly, the events on the continent in the 1930s seemed to point this way. Auden became increasingly interested in the idea of "The Leader" and, with his lifelong friend Christopher Isherwood, he explored the nature of leadership in a play, *The Ascent of F6* (1936). F6 is a mountain in border territory between a British colony and the state of Ostnia. The British government is determined to add F6 to the Empire by sending an expedition to climb and claim it. The leader is to be Michael Ransom. Although pressurized by the British government, it is really to gain the approval of his dominating mother that Ransom finally accepts the risks. Auden's point is that the public leader, the hero who climbs the mountain, is often taking on a public role to compensate for private weakness. The leader is not a truly great man but often a truly weak one, trying to overcome his insecurities by a dramatic piece of action. Auden remained sceptical, therefore, of any form of dictatorship, right or left, because he did not feel the leader, obsessed by private worries, could be working selflessly for the public good.

34 Fighting in the Spanish Civil War. It was marked by brutality on both sides.

In 1936 the Spanish Civil War broke out and Auden felt he must go to observe what appeared to be the crucial battle between the forces of tyranny and those of freedom. As he told a friend:

I am not one of those who believe that poetry need or even should be directly political, but in a critical period such as ours, I do believe that the poet must have direct knowledge of major political events. . . . Academic knowledge is not enough.

Auden left for Spain in January 1937 and spent two months there. His original plan seems to have been to become an ambulance driver, but he never achieved this. He spent most of his time in Barcelona which was the main Republican centre and which was run as a socialist society. Like many other foreign visitors, Auden was depressed by what he found. Instead of the forces of the left standing united in freedom, there were almost as many tensions between different groups of the left as there were between the left and its enemies, the Nationalists. "The politics were particularly unpleasant," he wrote later, and again, "Just seeing the Civil War was a shock. Nothing good could come out of it." He was particularly disturbed, in a way he had not expected to be, by the destruction of churches.

Auden continued to see himself as an anti-fascist and, in fact, he was seen by his contemporaries as a leading figure of the left. In no way, however, could he be said to be enthusiastic about the alternatives put forward by the left. Not only was he pessimistic about the future, he too much enjoyed his individual freedom, to work, to travel, to develop his ideas without restriction, ever to be a committed member of a single political party. Nevertheless, his visit to Spain inspired one of his finest political poems, *Spain 1937*. In this poem he looks back through history at some of the major achievements of mankind, "the invention of cartwheels and clocks, the taming of horses, the installation of dynamos and turbines, the construction of railways in the colonial desert". But at this point in history, the vital issue is "the struggle". "The struggle" is taking place in Spain. The call of her peoples for help is going out through the world. "Many have heard it on remote peninsulas, on sleepy plains, in the aberrant fisherman's islands, in the corrupt heart of the city" and they have come to Spain ("that fragment nipped off from Africa, soldered so crudely to inventive Europe") to "present their lives". They accept that by doing so they may themselves die, and that, in order to win the struggle, they may have to kill. What will be the result of their commitment? Here Auden is not so clear. It seems to be the maintenance of a society where people can live untroubled private lives. He talks of "the rediscovery of romantic life, all the fun under Liberty's masterful shadow, the walks by the lake, the winter of perfect communion". For Auden, an unrestricted private life was more important than one of public political commitment.

For Auden the visit to Spain appears to have been a profoundly depressing experience and the poetry he wrote in the months that followed was bitter. Perhaps he had never seen a major public role for the poet. In 1935, writing in the Introduction to a school anthology of poetry, *The Poet's Tongue*, he had argued that it was not the main job of the poet to persuade people what to do. It is rather to extend our knowledge of good and evil, "perhaps making the necessity for action more

35 W.H. Auden (right) sets off to view the war between China and Japan, January 1938. With him is his lifelong friend, Christopher Isherwood.

Mad Ireland hurt you into poetry,
Now Ireland has her madness and her weather
  still,
For poetry makes nothing happen.

Unresolved about his role as poet, and with no real hope for the future of Europe, Auden made the decision to leave for the United States. As Humphrey Carpenter puts it in his biography of Auden,

He turned to America, not because he had any dream of it as a perfect society but because he regarded it as a place where the options were still open and where no set pattern of civilization had yet been defined.

In January 1939, still only thirty-one, Auden set off with his friend Christopher Isherwood. A new life did lie abroad. Auden's most sustained love affair, with Chester Kalman, lay ahead, as well as a vigorous development of his poetry and other writings. In his later years, Auden returned to England, to his old college, Christ Church, Oxford. He died in 1973.

urgent and its nature more clear, but only leading us to the point where it is possible for us to make a rational and moral choice." In 1939, writing on the death of the great Irish poet, W.B. Yeats, and considering the impact he had made on Ireland, he commented:

George Orwell (1903-50)

Although George Orwell is perhaps best remembered for his two major works of the 1940s, *Animal Farm* and *1984*, it was in the 1930s that he first gained a reputation as a writer. A complex, often bitter, often lonely man, uneasy in personal relationships and distrustful of authority, Orwell felt a compulsive need to express his feelings about the world around him. In his novels of this period, he portrays the cramping effects of poverty on lower middle-class life. At the same time, he was exploring life at the bottom of British society, among tramps and in the depressed industrial towns. His records of his experiences provide a vivid picture of the decade.

Orwell was born Eric Blair in India in 1903. (He took the name Orwell soon after he began

In 1927 Orwell resigned his post and returned to England.

It was now that he decided to become a writer. At first, he had no literary skills. One of his acquaintances, the poet Ruth Pitter, later remembered his early efforts. "He wrote so badly. He had to teach himself writing, he was like a cow with a musket; it was sheer hard grind." Orwell persevered. Somehow, he needed to express the very deep emotions that Burma had brought out in him. "I was conscious of an immense weight of guilt I had to expiate," he wrote some years later.

I suppose that sounds exaggerated; but if you do for five years a job that you thoroughly disapprove of, you will probably feel the same. . . . I felt that I had got to escape not merely from imperialism but from every form of man's dominion over man. I wanted to submerge myself, to get right down among the oppressed; to be one of them and on their side against the tyrants.

This revealing confession explains much of what followed. Orwell "dropped out". He went to live in Paris and when his money ran out, took to washing dishes. Back in England he decided to become a tramp. In his first published book, *Down and Out in Paris and London* (1933), he tells of his experiences. In one passage he describes the effect of changing into tramp's clothing:

My new clothes had put me instantly in a new world. Everyone's demeanour seemed to have changed abruptly. I helped a hawker pick up a barrow he had upset. 'Thanks, Mate,' he said with a grin. No one had called me mate before in my life – it was the clothes that had done it. For the first time I noticed, too, how the attitude of women varies with a man's clothes. When a badly-dressed man passes them they shudder away from him with a quite frank movement of disgust, as though he was a dead cat. Clothes are powerful things . . .

Orwell found a kind of pleasure in "slumming

writing.) His father, a minor official of the British Empire, was an Opium Inspector. The family was soon split. Orwell, his mother and elder sister returned to England in 1904 and his father did not rejoin them until he retired several years later. It does not appear to have been a very affectionate family and Orwell emerged as a loner, seldom at ease with others.

He won a scholarship to Eton, and when the time came for him to leave there, he avoided university and decided that he would return to the East. He found a post as a policeman in Burma. It was not a fortunate choice. Orwell always hated institutions; now he had to uphold the authority of one, the British Empire. He later described his memories of the beaten prisoners and the tears of their families as they were led away into captivity.

Things like that are beyond bearing when you are in any way responsible for them. I once saw a man hanged. It seemed to be worse than a thousand murders. I never went into a jail without feeling that my place was on the other side of the bars. (*The Road to Wigan Pier*)

37 George Orwell brought home to many the nature of poverty in the Britain of the thirties. These are backyards in Shoreditch in London. Note the washing drying in the grimy atmosphere.

it". As another of his friends recalled,

he seemed to think of himself as a rebel – which, or course, he was. I mean he questioned middle-class values all the time and wanted to identify himself with a more working class background, but I don't think he could ever quite make it.

Many of Orwell's acquaintances of these years felt his sense of not belonging. "I would have said he was an unhappy man," Geoffrey Gorer, a friend from this time, has commented.

He was too big for himself. . . . He was awfully likely to knock things off tables, to trip over things. I mean, he was a gangling physically badly coordinated young man . . . he was a lonely man . . . a very lonely man. He was fairly well convinced that nobody would like him which made him prickly.

Many of Orwell's frustrations are clearly expressed in his first important novel *Keep the Aspidistra Flying** (1936). Here, Orwell's

*The aspidistra is a pot plant used here as a symbol of middle-class life.

theme is poverty. The "hero", Gordon Comstock, is, as Orwell himself was for some time in the thirties, an assistant in a bookshop, trying at the same time to be a writer. He is obsessed with his own sense of failure and even more by the narrow and gloomy life which is all his £2 a week salary can bring him. His poverty poisons everything, not least his relationship with Rosemary, who earns more than he does but from whom he refuses to borrow. He is particularly bitter towards the money gods who control so many people's lives:

He had a vision of London, of the western world; he saw a thousand million slaves toiling and grovelling about the throne of money. The earth is ploughed, ships sail, miners sweat in dripping tunnels underground, clerks hurry for the eight-fifteen with the fear of the boss eating at their vitals. And even in bed with their wives they tremble and obey. Obey whom? The money priesthood, the pinfaced masters of the world. The Upper Crust.

The air of gloom pervades the book. One evening Gordon is walking through the streets of London with his friend Ravelston.

They were walking southward down a darkish, meanly decent residential street with a few shuttered shops. From a hoarding on the blank end of a house the yard wide face of Corner Table simpered, pallid in the lamplight. Gordon caught a glimpse of a withering aspidistra in a lower window. London! Mile after mile of mean lonely houses, let off in flats and single rooms; not homes, not communities, just clusters of meaningless lives drifting in a sort of drowsy chaos to the grave.

It is only gradually that Gordon does find some sort of hope, when Rosemary becomes pregnant and they decide to get married. Gordon recognizes that there is some kind of

38 A street in Wigan – the town whose plight was publicized in Orwell's *The Road to Wigan Pier*.

future in marriage, fatherhood and middle-class conformity.

It was in the mid-1930s that Orwell's exasperations began to be transformed into political beliefs. In 1936 the socialist publisher, Victor Gollancz offered to finance him to make a trip north to bring back an account of what life in depressed England really was like. Orwell spent two months in the North, most of the time in Wigan, a town which had depended on both coal and cotton for its livelihood. Orwell's description of everyday life there, the struggle to make ends meet, the effects of the Means Test and the desolation of a depressed area make *The Road to Wigan Pier* (1937) one of the most important social documents of the decade. An extract is given on page 61.

In the second part of the book Orwell develops his own political views. He starts by recalling his own upbringing, concentrating on the class system which he feels dominates the English way of life. Somehow, this system has to be broken down so that a fairer and more humane way of life can emerge. The only way that this can be done, Orwell believes, is by building a broad-based socialist movement which is centred on a few clearly defined values.

There are, I believe, countless people who without being aware of it, are in sympathy with the essential aims of socialism, and who could be won over almost without a struggle if only one could find the word that would move them.

Everyone who knows the meaning of poverty, everyone who has a genuine hatred of tyranny and war, is on the socialist side potentially.

One of the obstacles to the building of a socialist movement, says Orwell, is the narrowness of so many left-wing parties, with their obsessions with detail and "correct attitudes".

Orwell felt that time was running out for the hopes of socialism.

In the next few years we shall either get that effective socialist party that we need, or we shall not get it. If we do not get it then fascism is coming. . . .

His fears were confirmed by the outbreak of the Spanish Civil War. For Orwell this was the turning point.

Every line of serious work that I have written since 1936 has been written directly or indirectly against totalitarianism and for democratic socialism as I understand it.

When he heard the news that there had been a coup against the Spanish Republican Government Orwell decided he must go to fight for the Republicans. "This fascism," he told a friend, in his direct way, "somebody's got to stop it."

39 The International Brigade, sympathizers of the Republican cause in Spain, who left Britain to offer support. Orwell joined them and was wounded in the civil war.

There were a number of political groups in Spain which organized their own militias in defence of the Republic. The largest was controlled by the Spanish trade union movement. The best equipped were the Communists, who received supplies and direction from Russia. Orwell joined the United Marxist Workers Party (P.O.U.M., as it was known, from the initials of its Spanish title), one of the smallest groups. Unlike many other visitors to Spain, Orwell actually fought, spending some time on an, admittedly quiet, part of the front line. Later, he went to Barcelona, and, while he was there, fighting broke out between the Communists and the P.O.U.M. The left, supposedly united against the Nationalists, was, in fact, turning on itself. Orwell had never been close to the Communists, but their activities in Spain turned him bitterly against them. He particularly despised the way they twisted language in such a way as to discredit their opponents. The P.O.U.M., for instance, most of whose members were totally dedicated to the cause, were denounced as "fascists". In his later works, *1984* and *Animal Farm*, Orwell was to develop this theme.

On returning to the front line in May 1937, Orwell was wounded and finally returned to England. It was a depressing time. Italy had crushed Abyssinia in 1935-6. Hitler had been allowed to expand eastward with, at the Munich Agreement of September 1938, the active support of Britain. In 1939, the Republican Government in Spain was finally defeated. There was a general feeling that war was now inevitable. For Orwell, war was to be hated not just for the bloodshed it brought but because he felt that it would encourage authoritarianism in Britain, the emergence of British fascism to fight continental fascism.

Orwell's last novel before war broke out, *Coming Up For Air* (1939), is full of the gloom of impending disaster. George Bowling, an insurance clerk, living in a lower middle-class suburb of appalling sterility (see page 56) decides to visit the village where he was brought up. It is as if he wants to find his real roots before everything is destroyed. Images of war dominate. As Bowling travels by train, sitting opposite some commercial travellers, he notices a bomber flying alongside the train.

The great black bombing plane swayed a little in the air and zoomed ahead so that I couldn't see it. One of the commercials cocked his eye at it for just a second. I knew what he was thinking. You don't have to be a highbrow to have such thoughts nowadays. In two years' time, one year's time, what shall we be doing when we see one of those things? Making a dive for the cellar, wetting our bags with fright.

When Bowling eventually reaches his home village, it has been destroyed by modern development. Even his roots have died.

Orwell's work is not always enjoyable to read. He was, in many ways, a bitter man. How much this came from his childhood experiences and how much from Burma is difficult to say. He was, however, deeply honest, always determined to present his own view, free of influence of any movement, whether literary or political. This is what gives his work its strength and what makes him such an important figure of the 1930s. He was prepared to commit himself totally, not only to his work but also to the active fulfilment of his political beliefs. This was a rare combination and deserves to be recognized.

"The People"

In the 1930s Britain remained an unequal but very ordered society. In fact, its political and social stability in these years was quite remarkable. The Depression and the years that followed were weathered with virtually no resort to political extremism of either the right or the left. People got on with life, preoccupied with their worries and insecurities, but seldom seeking political solutions for them.

The contrasts in living standards, as the following "lives" will show, were extraordinary. At one extreme we find Chips Channon, noting in his diary in September 1935, "It is very difficult to spend less than £200 a morning when one goes out shopping." At the other we find Nancy Sharman, unable to spend 2½d on a loaf of fresh bread and waiting until one is sold off more cheaply, a day later.

Relationships were still authoritarian, particularly between master and servant. Christopher Falconer recalls in *Akenfield* his years of service as a gardener in a "big house":

Lord and Ladyship were very, very Victorian and very domineering. It was 'swing your arms' every time they saw us. Ladyship would appear suddenly from nowhere when one of us boys were walking off to fetch something. 'Swing your arms!' she would shout. . . . Nobody was allowed to smoke. A gardener was sacked immediately if he was caught smoking, no matter how long he had worked there.

Many communities, especially those in rural areas, were still very isolated and it was only slowly that the cinema, radio and, perhaps most important, health services penetrated the country. These were years of improvement, but the gaps left by the social services and the spreading of prosperity were still large. The struggle to survive, symbolized by the struggle of many to keep homes and bodies clean, was a very real one for the majority of the population.

Virtually every memoir of the period tells how events in Europe, at first ignored, gradually came to play an ever more prominent part in life as the decade continued. In 1936, Churchill, writing in the *Evening Standard*, issued a warning:

One looks at the people going about their daily round, crowding the streets on their business, earning their livelihood, filling the football grounds and the cinemas. One reads their newspapers, always full of entertaining headlines whether the happenings are great or small. Do they realise the way events are trending? And how external forces may affect all their work and pleasure, all their happiness, all their freedom, all their property and all whom

40 The FA Cup Tie, 1936, Arsenal versus Barnsley. The nation's obsession with football helped to keep minds off the gathering war clouds in Europe.

they love? I can only see one thing. I see it sharper and harsher day by day. Germany is arming more strenuously, more scientifically and upon a larger scale, than any other nation armed before.

It was the Munich crisis of 1938 and then Hitler's invasion of Czechoslovakia in March 1939 which finally brought home to the British public how serious the situation was.

When war did come Britain faced it as a united nation. What Orwell described as Britain's "emotional unity, that tendency of nearly all its inhabitants to feel alike and act together in moments of supreme crisis", played its part in Britain's victory. But when that victory came and "the people" had the chance to vote, they rejected the Conservative Party which had led them in the previous decade, and voted in a Labour Government.

Chips Channon (1897-1958)

The 1930s saw the last years of the glittering world of London society. A small elite, of perhaps six hundred people, was the centre of an extravagant and colourful succession of balls, dinners and country house parties. London society was still dominated by the older aristocratic families, but beauty, money, even the talent to amuse could provide an admission ticket. Some hostesses, such as Laura Corrigan, had arrived from America, knowing no-one, but prepared to spend lavishly for their eventual acceptance. Popular songwriters, such as Cole Porter or Noel Coward, were welcomed. One newcomer to London society was Chips Channon, a wealthy American who had fallen in love with English life. His diaries of these years give an excellent picture not only of society life but also of the political dramas which overshadowed its final days.

Chips Channon was born in Chicago in 1897. His family had made a fortune from shipping on the Great Lakes and their wealth enabled Chips to live in style for the rest of his life. He had first come to Europe in 1910, to spend three months in a school in Paris, and in 1917 returned to France to work with the American Red Cross. Almost at once, he seems to have been accepted in French society, quickly intimate with both writers and duchesses. In 1918 he made his first visit

to London and realized that here his future lay. He was to die forty years later, Sir Henry Channon, owner of a country house in Essex, Kelvedon, which he described as "a dream of loveliness".

Chips spent his first years in England as an undergraduate at Oxford and he seems to have moved from there almost immediately into London society. He clearly had an enormous talent for friendship; his money alone could not have gained him such immediate acceptance. Lady Diana Cooper, one of the most celebrated figures of society in these years, has written of him:

41 Chips Channon marries Lady Honor Guinness at the fashionable St. Margarets, Westminster, July 1933.

42 The Circus Ball at Grosvenor House, 1933. Chips, on the right, is seen with Diana Cooper, one of the leading members of London society and Cecil Beaton, the fashionable photographer.

never was there a surer or more enlivening friend. . . . He installed the mighty in his gilded chairs and exalted the humble. He made the old and tired, the young and strong, shine beneath his thousand lighted candles. Without stint he gave of his riches and of his compassion.

In 1933 Chips married Lady Honor Guinness, the daughter of the Earl of Iveagh, and they bought a large house in fashionable Belgrave Square. It was decorated sumptuously, with the dining room a copy of the famous blue room in the Amalienburg Palace near Munich. Here the Channons entertained in style.

The guests at 5 Belgrave Square tended to be a bewildering but carefully blended mixture of politicians, diplomats, royalties, soldiers, publishers, authors, courtiers and – particularly in later years – actors, actresses and theatrical

producers. (Robert Rhodes James, *Introduction to the Channon Diaries*)

Chips' career was not just that of a leading host. In 1935 he "inherited" the Conservative seat of Southend-on-Sea which had been held by both his father and mother-in-law and which, on his death in 1958, was to pass, in turn, to his son Paul. Chips spoke seldom in the House of Commons, but, as a very junior member of the Government (Parliamentary Private Secretary to the Under-Secretary of State for Foreign Affairs, Rab Butler), he had access to much political gossip.

The world in which Chips moved was certainly glittering. In May 1937, he describes a dinner party he and Honor gave before the Duchess of Sutherland's ball.

A dazzling night. Honor looked magnificent with all her sapphires, tiara and a resplendent blue brocade number made to match the Amalienburg and we were hardly dressed and down before that brace of princelings, Ernst August of Hanover and Fritzy of Prussia, very young, fair and Nordic and dripping with decorations, arrived almost too punctually. Soon after nine we swept into dinner, and the dining room was a gorgeous, glittering sight of jewels shimmering in the candle-light, of Meissen china, of decorations and splendour.

Chips confessed himself "rivetted . . . by glamour, society and jewels". On one occasion, "Lady Granard could scarcely walk for jewels". On another, Chips found himself sitting next to Wallis Simpson, now closely involved with the King, Edward VIII. "She was wearing new jewels – the King must give her new ones every day." The greatest moment of all came at the Coronation of George VI in 1937. As Chips looked around at the scene in Westminster Abbey, he could see his mother-in-law,

on the Countesses' bench who looked magnificent as her glorious diamond rivière made a circle of blazing light. It sparkled as she moved . . . the North Transept was a vitrine of bosoms and jewels and bobbing tiaras. . . . The

43 1930. A reception at Buckingham Palace for debutantes. Miss Wilma Palmer-Chapman arrives in style.

loveliest moment of all [was the] swirl when the Peeresses put on their coronets: a thousand white gloved arms, sparkling with jewels, lifting their tiny coronets.

Between these occasions, the Channons found peace in weekends in country houses. One of Chips' favourites was Sutton Courtenay, the home of the hostess Norah Lindsay. In June 1936 Chips writes:

We came to this floral, lovely paradise, world worn and nerve shattered. But a few hours here, and we were both once more ourselves. The smell of the roses, the lapping of the water, the colours and above all Norah's tremendous charm and personality work wonders. . . . We had dinner in the courtyard, and Norah played the piano. There was scent, sensuousness, simplicity, serenity, and finally sleep.

What a house Sutton Courtenay is. For two generations it has moulded the youth of England, it has seen them go forth into battle and into the world; all must have carried away memories of bathing in its Thames backwater, of reading poetry in the rose garden, of cutting trees and gardening, of listening to and loving Norah Lindsay.

Chips could not help becoming involved in the great social and political drama caused by the King's infatuation with Wallis Simpson. Chips met Wallis Simpson frequently in 1935 and 1936; she and the King were invited out quite openly together. "I grew to admire and

like her," wrote Chips.

She is a woman of charm, sense, balance and great wit, with dignity and taste. She has always been an excellent influence on the King who has loved her honestly and openly. I really consider she would have made an excellent Queen.

Chips appears to have hoped that the King could make a morganatic marriage, one in which Wallis Simpson would have become his wife but would not have had the full status as Queen. Such a solution was not considered possible and Chips was in the House of Commons to hear the King's final decision.

The House was full for there had not been an Abdication since 1399, 537 years ago. I thought everyone subdued and surprisingly unmoved. . . . Baldwin was greeted with cheers, and sat down on the front bench gravely. At last he went to the bar, bowed twice 'A Message From the King' and presented a paper to the Speaker who read it out. At the words 'renounce the throne' his voice broke and there were stifled sobs in the House.

In the next three years politics dominated Chips' life. At heart, he was deeply conservative and a passionate supporter of the existing order. He was also, at first, sympathetic to Nazi Germany and he and Honor paid a visit there in August 1936. They were the guests of many of the Nazi leaders. "Goering, wreathed in smiles and orders and decorations, received us gaily, his wife at his side" at one "dazzling crowded function". The Goerings were, however, outdone by the Goebbels (Josef Goebbels was Hitler's Propaganda Minister), who had thrown a bridge over to an island and invited two thousand people to a festival which ended with cannons and fireworks.

Back in London, Chips became a fervent supporter of the appeasement policy. He felt that a settlement could and should be achieved by Britain and Germany. He developed a sort of hero-worship for Neville Chamberlain. During the Munich crisis, as Chamberlain set off for yet another meeting with Hitler, Chips wrote:

I will always remember little Neville today, with his too long hair, greying at the sides, his smile, his amazing spirits and his seeming lack of fatigue, as he stood there, alone fighting the dogs of war [i.e. those like Winston Churchill who felt that Hitler must be confronted not appeased] single-handed and triumphant – he seemed the reincarnation of St George – so simple and so unspoiled – now in a few hours for the third time he takes a plane to a far country in the service of England. May God speed him and reward him for his efforts.

Sadly, Chips' devotion to the Prime Minister was misplaced. Chamberlain was following his course blindly and almost without advice from his own Foreign Office. Within a few months of the Munich Agreement, Hitler's true intentions of conquest to the East had become apparent. Chips was as deeply disillusioned as the rest, though he continued to give his support to Chamberlain. On 22 August 1939, the news came that Russia had made a secret pact with Germany, leaving Germany free to attack Poland. Savouring the summer at his lovely country house, Kelvedon, Chips wrote:

I feel that a new era, perhaps the last, has opened for England and incidentally for me. It began this quiet, sunlit morning when I sleepily opened the newspaper and read emblazoned across the ever sensational Express 'German-Russian Pact'. Then I realised that the Russians have double-crossed us, as I always believed they would. . . . Now it looks like war . . .

Only ten days later Chips' fears were to come true.

Just the month before, Chips had been a guest at one of the last great social occasions of the thirties, a summer ball at Blenheim Palace, the home of the Duke of Marlborough.

[It] was stupendous. I have seen much, travelled far and am accustomed to splendour, but there has never been anything like tonight. The palace was floodlit, and its grand baroque beauty could be seen for miles. The lakes were floodlit too and, better still, the famous terraces, they were blue and green and Tyroleans walked about singing; and although there were seven hundred people or even more, it was not in the least crowded. It was gay, young, brilliant, in short, perfection. I was loath to leave, but did so at about 4.30 and took one last look at the baroque terraces with the lake below, and the golden statues and the great palace. Shall we see the like again? Is such a function not out of date? Yet it was all of the England that is supposed to be dead and is not. There were literally rivers of champagne.

Now this world was fading. The great houses were to be closed up or converted into hospitals or military headquarters. When the lights could go up again in 1945, Britain was under a socialist government and London society never recovered its former glamour.

Richard Cobb (b. 1917)

Until 1984 Richard Cobb was Professor of History at Oxford University. He is, without doubt, the leading British historian of the French Revolution. His achievement as a historian has been to look beyond the public events of the Revolution to the private dramas behind them. It is as if he can go back to the street corners of Paris nearly two hundred years ago and watch how individuals, both rich and poor, came to terms with the turmoil

of the Revolution. In his book *Still Life*, he brings the same qualities to a study of Tunbridge Wells between the wars. Here, however, the individuals he watched as a child are seen in a timeless and uneventful world, vastly different from that of Revolutionary France.

As a guide book of 1923 puts it,

Tunbridge Wells is never overrun with trippers, nor are its streets ever defiled by the vulgar or the inane. Its inhabitants are composed for the most part of well-to-do people who naturally create social atmosphere tinged with culture and refinement.

The Tunbridge Wells of the 1930s that Richard Cobb describes seemed to exist apart from the real world. It was true that many of its middle-class inhabitants hurried off on the morning train to the City, but for most of this class life was lived almost entirely within the town. Few had been born there. They had retired on private incomes or come to spend their last years after a lifetime in the service of the British Empire. Richard Cobb's father had been in the Sudan. One block of flats was reserved for widows of army officers, civil

44 Tunbridge Wells in the 1930s, middle-class life at its most respectable.

servants or railway officials returned from India (Richard Cobb imagined, rather romantically, that their husbands had been eaten by tigers). Life revolved round the clubs, bridge, tennis or golf. Social life was conducted according to strict and unvarying conventions, quickly learned and adhered to by all those who wished to belong.

To Richard Cobb as a child, life in Tunbridge Wells seemed timeless. It was as if the conventions of Edwardian England had stretched on, mingling with, but often over-ruling, those of the twenties and thirties. Some inhabitants appeared in clothes which had clearly been made for the summer seasons of many years before. One ancient Edwardian car, complete with chauffeur, lasted right through to the 1940s. For Cobb, this unchanging way of life was symbolized by people. There was Miss Amy Lake, who ran an infant school. Her clothes dated from the early 1900s . . .

even the large man's umbrella that she always prudently carried, in all seasons, the moulting

4
DOUBLE
BEDROOMS
3
RECEPTION
ROOMS
LOUNGE HALL
BIG CAR
GARAGE
FITTED KITCHEN
BATHROOM
CLOAKROOM

———

FOR FREE
PLANS

contained in fully illus-
trated Book, simply sign
below, pin to your letter-
heading and post in un-
sealed envelope addressed:
Richard Costain, Ltd.
(Builders for 70 Years),
Costain House, Upper
Woburn Place, London,
W.C.1. (½d Stamp only).

Name ....
D.T.24.1.36

JUST A TROT TO

EPSOM DOWNS

and SURREY'S RIDING COUNTRY

Why be tied to suburban environment ? Here are new recreative outlets,
refreshing rural interests, at your very door. Cheap hack-riding over miles of
high, open downland ; golf within a few minutes' walk ; open-road motoring
from your garage gates onwards to coast and country.

Yet from Kingswood Station, or Tadworth (10 minutes' walk), your London
office is within 40 minutes.

Here, too, is the home which is a compliment to your demands for something distinctive in design—with that *fourth* double-sized bedroom which you
need, maybe to accommodate the maid that you *don't really need* in

The TEAKWOOD HOME

(10 minutes from KINGSWOOD and TADWORTH STATIONS)

ACCESSIBLE SECLUSION

is offered in this heathland home, so adequately proportioned, so beautifully built. To
SEE the Costain-built Teakwood Home is to realise the futility of printed description.
There have been very few who have viewed this home and have not bought it. The
Book of the Teakwood Home, which includes Plans and profuse illustrations, reveals
qualities that will invite you, too, to turn out and inspect it.

£1,180 *to* £1,225   FREEHOLD
INCLUSIVE
(According to plot size)

Three minutes after passing Burgh Heath on the main Brighton Road going south, turn
right. By rail to Kingswood Station (S.R. from Charing X or London Bridge), Estate
Office outside Station. Car waiting.

45 New homes on offer, 1936. Better transport by
road and rail are making middle-class commuting
much more attractive.

black fur around her neck, and the huge leather bag, attached to her arm, seemed changeless. She always shopped in the nearby Pantiles, accompanied by a little black, white and brown fox-terrier – she must have got through at least half-a-dozen during the period that I knew her – on a lead. Her shopping proceeded likewise in a changeless sequence, no doubt adopted in pre-war days, Dust's, for hat-pins and buttons, Durrant's, for dog-food, Porter's for the replacement of rubber balls and other essential toys, Charlton's, for rhubarb and vegetables . . . a pause at the bandstand, if the band were playing . . . and finally, a visit to Jupp's, at the end of the Pantiles, where she replenished her stocks of mild snuff and took on board a huge bag of further supplies of sweets for her pupils.

Perhaps even more remarkable were Cobb's cousins, the Limbury-Buses, father and mother, unmarried son and daughter, both in their thirties in the 1930s, who kept up an unchanging ritual of life for several decades.

Geoff [the son] went out every day at two, carrying a shopping bag, and dressed, like my father, in an oatmeal jacket and plus-fours. His route was invariable: past the Kent and Sussex hospital, then along the Common, past Thackeray's house, a purchase at Romary's biscuit shop, thence to the Kent and Sussex Club. As he moved with majestic slowness, he would not reach the Club till 2.30. After playing a rubber or two of bridge, he would have tea at the Club, then a single sherry; home by the same route, for 6.30.

In the early 1950s, Cobb, back temporarily from Paris, "sighted Geoff, at the correct time, at the Romary's Water Biscuits Halt." Ten years later, he could be spotted again, exactly on time.

Life in middle-class Tunbridge Wells was dominated by conventions. Each road had its own social status, and so new arrivals could be quickly assessed. There were parts of the town where it was unsuitable for its middle-class inhabitants to go or to be seen, and parents no doubt magnified the "dangers" of these areas to their children. Cobb writes:

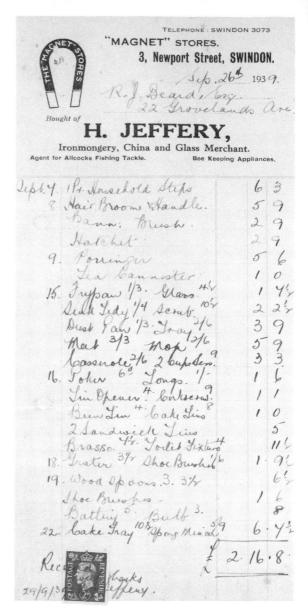

46 Shopping in the thirties. Better-off families would have an account with local shops and settle their bills once a month.

I was always afraid of High Brooms, and of the people who lived there, and I was rather afraid of the upper reaches of Upper Grosvenor Road, though, at 12, I summoned up enough courage to penetrate it *almost* to the bottom.

Even the High Street had its more fashionable side:

It was on the *north* side that my mother met her friends, ladies in sensible hats, tweed suits,

Jaeger jerseys, baskets and heavy shoes, with dogs on leads, and stopped at a series of gossiping posts, a dozen or more: the Nevill Bakery, the better chemist, Payne's, the silversmith, Goulden and Curry, the coffee shop which also sold expensive chocolates, and smelt of both, the butcher's, a dress-shop, and, at the far end, a bank.

The barriers between public and private life were very clearly drawn. You could never visit anyone socially before three o'clock and even then there were limits on those who could be visited. For the Cobbs, most of the neighbouring houses remained totally unknown.

47 A typical middle-class home of the 1930s. This is the home of the novelist Warwick Deeping.

For well over thirty years, the uneven line of lighted windows facing us across Claremont Road at roughly the level of our kitchen or our dining room never revealed anything of the slightest interest . . . not one single glimpse of domestic life, even momentarily revealed. My mother would know the names of 'the people living opposite'; she would even know what they did, how many children and animals they had, whether or not they had a car. She might even greet them in the street. But that would be as far as it would go.

With so much hidden from view, a penetration into a home became an adventure. One never knew what to expect. Once, Richard Cobb found himself summoned to tea by a Mr Evans, an invalid, who lived in "a dark mysterious house". Admitted by an elderly maid, and taken into the house, he was shown through to a dining room.

I had never seen an array as magnificent as that which confronted me on Mr. Evans' enormous dining room table: a thick, glistening stiff white table cloth on which two places were laid, Mr. Evans's at the head of the table, and mine on his right facing the dark wintry garden. By each there were two lots of big cups in flower patterns, three silver knives and three silver forks. In front of Mr. Evans's place stood, like ungainly storks, a pair of huge silver teapots, with little silver taps, as well as long, graceful spouts, each on a tall

stand, and under which burnt a bluish flame. The rest of the table was strewn with tiered edifices like miniature pagodas, also in silver and supporting from a series of branches, plates of thinly cut sandwiches, muffins, crumpets, scones, a chocolate cake, a cherry cake, a seed cake, an iced cake, and a yellow cake with cream and jam filling.

Cobb was then introduced by Mr. Evans to his outstanding collection of early English watercolours.

So many of the "real" events of life in Tunbridge Wells were never mentioned in polite conversation that Richard Cobb had to rely on other sources for gossip. The hairdresser was an excellent source, so was Dr Rankin, whose father and grandfather had been Tunbridge Wells doctors before him. Dr Rankin was only four feet tall and he had to carry a stool with him on his rounds so that he could clamber up to inspect his bedridden patients. He told Cobb that the best patients were those with nothing the matter with them and for whom "the weekly visit from their doctor represented a social event to be looked forward to".

In this world, Cobb, a shy boy, developed his own way of life. He spent much time following different walks around the town, especially across its green spaces. Each different walk brought its own atmosphere and associations. In his imagination he came to believe that a revolution might take place against this ordered and complacent world and he increasingly came to rely on the unchanging pace of life for his own security. It was seeing the same people, following the same pattern of life year after year that made Tunbridge Wells a haven to return to later in his life.

Of course, the real world at last caught up with the town.

On a dreadful day in September 1939 my mother and I were sitting in deckchairs on the flat roof. It might have been ten or thereabouts, when Mrs Martin [their cleaning lady] came up saying: 'The Germans are at them Poles, Ma'am.' I felt as if I had swallowed a huge lump of ice. The Wellington, the Earl's Court, the Regency houses of the top dentists and the tower of Rusthall Church and the rest of Mount Ephraim all remained in place, everything *looked* just the same; but nothing could *ever* be the same. Politics were getting too close to Tunbridge Wells.

As a final and unforgivable outrage, the Germans even dropped bombs on the town.

Most of these bombs destroyed large middle-class houses and their inhabitants, including the resident servants, in such respectable areas as Lansdowne Road. I recall one large yellow house . . . that had been cut right down one side, revealing the flowered wall-papers of drawing room, dining room and hall, all familiar to me because the house belonged to one of my mother's Bridge friends . . . what seemed most horrifying was this breach of privacy, the indecent exposure of what had never been supposed to have been seen: the inside of bedrooms, the patterns of their wall-paper.

Here, indeed, for Tunbridge Wells, was the ultimate indignity.

The thirties in Tunbridge Wells do not stand out as a distinct period for Richard Cobb. Too much of life was simply a continuation of patterns set years, perhaps decades, before. The middle-class inhabitants, secure with their pensions or private incomes, did not have to adapt. Perhaps never again would a class be able to live so isolated from the realities of life.

John Osborne (b. 1929) and Philip Oakes (b. 1928)

In his novel *Coming Up For Air*, George Orwell describes a typical lower middle-class housing estate of the 1930s. The "hero" of the book, George Bowling, has come to settle with his wife and two children in Ellesmere Road, West Bletchley, on the outskirts of London. "Do you know the road I live in?" he asks.

Even if you don't, you know fifty others exactly like it . . . you know how the streets fester all over the inner-outer suburbs. Always the same, long, long rows of little semi-detached houses.

It was not only the drab uniformity of the roads which worried Bowling. It was also the fear.

We are all in the middle of paying for our houses and eaten up with the ghastly fear that something might happen before we've made the last payment.

The picture painted by Orwell is one of precarious respectability. The inhabitants of the Ellesmere-type Roads have escaped from

48 Ribbon development – new factories, new roads, new homes – the spread of thirties Britain.

49 Home from work – relaxing in one of the new homes.

the slums of the cities or avoided the council estates. There is just a chance that, after years of paying their mortgages, they might actually own their homes. They are terrified of falling backwards, losing what little independence and comfort they have achieved. In two autobiographies of childhood in this decade, the playwright, John Osborne, and the novelist and poet, Philip Oakes, describe their own experiences of life on these new estates.

John Osborne's father was a copywriter with an advertising agency. The family had started life in Fulham, but in the mid-thirties had moved out to Stoneleigh, one of many new developments on the Waterloo to Effingham Junction line. "Stoneleigh itself was a station surrounded by groups of housing estates," he recalls.

Coming off the concrete railway bridge on either side were 'Shopping Parades'. In the middle was the Stoneleigh Hotel, which was not a hotel at all but a by-pass Tudor pub. . . . The Parades consisted of a small Woolworth's, the dry cleaner's, newsagents and a twopenny library, butchers, florists and empty shops which had not yet been sold, gaps in the townscape, corners which had not yet been built on, patches of field and stubble between houses and shops. [At Stoneleigh] the developer's fingers hesitated briefly before ploughing onwards, and paused to spread haphazard speculative tentacles.

Beyond Stoneleigh were Ewell West and Epsom, a rather unappealing Victorian town being changed into a new, bright, brick and cemetery dormitory like others that became Reigate, Redhill, Leatherhead and Dorking. But beyond them lay the Downs; Effingham Junction nudged countryside which still had a few secrets left. (*A Better Class of Person*)

Philip Oakes in *From Middle England* describes this same mixture of new building and old countryside:

We lived in an avenue of pebble-dashed semis whose windows and leaded lights turned hopefully towards green fields . . . even after four years the estate had not been completed. Opposite our house was a patch we knew as The Waste. It was a safe playground, close to home but sufficiently private to light fires without being seen. Further afield was Banky Brook, a black oily stream running from Sneyd Green colliery, to be jumped at its widest part as an initiation rite, and a small marsh in which hundreds of frogs squatted, only the knobs of their eyes showing above the weeds.

This was in Burslem, one of the pottery towns.

The Oakes family had reached their status through education. Philip's grandfather had made wooden crates for pottery, but two of his nine children had worked themselves up to be teachers and one a civil engineer. When Philip, aged eight, complained of the family plan to send him away to school, he was quickly shut up.

Education raged through my mother's family like strong drink, the only intoxicant permitted by a brood of North Staffordshire Methodists whose philosophy of life was based on a set of gritty maxims in which Plain Living, High Thinking ran a close second to Waste Not, Want Not. . . . The drive and the impulse were both irresistable and

50 Burslem, a pottery town, in the 1930s. Many yearned to escape from the grime and smoke of the industrial town and for the first time could hope to do so.

51 The Hoover man comes to call. Electrical appliances revolutionized the fight against dirt.

Hundreds of Thousands

OF WOMEN

BLESS THE DAY THIS SALESMAN CALLED!

● Before they had the Hoover they were just like you—not particularly interested.

It was not till a Hoover man showed them the mass of dirt the Hoover took out of their *own* carpets — carpets they believed clean—that they *began* to realise their need of a Hoover.

Not one of them to-day would willingly be without the Hoover! Not one of them would willingly go back to the old time and energy-wasting ways.

Are you so very different from them? Isn't it true that you also would welcome such an inexpensive escape from drudgery?—Just 10/- down.

So when the Hoover man calls, give him a hearing! If you can't see him then, tell him when you can. Be fair to yourself and to him. See for yourself——let him show you . . . . . After all, hundreds of thousands of housewives can't be wrong, can they?

The **HOOVER**
REGISTERED TRADE MARK
I: BEATS ... *as it Sweeps* ... *as it Cleans*

FOR ONLY 10/- DOWN

COUPON to Hoover Ltd., Dept. W.1, Perivale, Greenford, Middlesex.
Please send me without obligation your booklet describing the new Hoovers.

NAME ....

ADDRESS ....

my feeble objection to going away to school was a kind of heresy.

Life on both estates seems to have been dominated by the fight to keep everything clean. "Every Friday was Black Friday," writes John Osborne,

the day when we had what was the Spring Clean. Sheets were draped over the furniture and chairs were piled on tables. Mattresses would be ripped from their beds, curtains taken down, washed and ironed. In the winter, when it was not possible to go outside, the Black Look clouding over the billowing dust bag of the Hoover was inescapable as it thrust its way into every corner, every bed or cupboard, bellowing and bullying a filthy uncomprehending world for hours. Handing over the Hoover to my mother was like distributing highly sophisticated nuclear weapons to an under-developed African nation. By early evening she would be almost babbling with fatigue. A breathless interval at midday allowed us to bolt down an egg on mashed potatoes, frenziedly washed up so that she could 'get on' for the rest of the afternoon and a final burst to clear the field of spotless battle and return everything to its gleaming, dustless place before my father returned home from work.

Philip Oakes remembers:

In my aunt's house, the grime was not allowed to settle. Sills were dusted. The kitchen table was scrubbed white. The radio, veneered in walnut, with a front fretted like a church window, was polished daily.

The picture given by both writers is one of a cramped way of life where endless lengths were gone to to keep up respectability. Very few social contacts were made but everybody watched everyone else – and had their own way of watching. Philip Oakes is waiting for the optician to call to see his mother.

I went to the front room from where I could watch for Mr Aaron's arrival. There were other watchers in the houses opposite. Mrs Royals kept observation from her spare bedroom. Occasionally the curtains would twitch and Mrs Royals' nose would edge into view as she followed the progress of the postman from house to house. Her neighbour, Mrs Sproston, kept watch through her front door, held slightly ajar, while Mrs Pointon monitored the comings and goings through the leaded lights of her lounge.

Most social contacts were with close family and both the Osbornes and the Oakes had many relations in the neighbourhood of their new homes. A common meeting time was Christmas, although the two families approached the festivities in a very different spirit. For Philip Oakes's mother, Christmas represented

the family united against the world; a time when slights were forgiven, bonds fortified.

For the Osbornes,

The highlight of Christmas was the Family Row. The common acrimony and bitterness of generations would claim its victims long before the Christmas wrappings had been thrown away . . . [Finally] two days of bewilderment, betrayal, triumph and, above all, irredeemable and incurable disappointment ended. My parents gathered up our presents. A redemptive after-battle calm settled over the sitting room strewn with wrapping paper and ribbon. We shuffled out in near silence back to Stoneleigh Park Road and my father's whisky bottle. Another Christmas Over.

Poverty did cramp lives on these estates and even the status symbols had to be used with care. John Osborne comments that

the few telephones, always beside the front door next to the coatstand in the hall, like an unwanted ornament or vacuum cleaner, can seldom have been used for idle conversation. Sited by the coldest draught with nowhere to sit, it was an instrument for discouraging communication, forbidding it in the interest of frugality of pocket and spirit, only to be used in the reporting of sickness, disaster or death.

There was the same sense of frugality in Philip Oakes's house, though there does not seem to have been the same obsession about money that many of Osborne's relations had. He remembers:

Rising prices and shoddy goods were constant themes in my mother's conversation with my aunts.

When the richer Aarons befriended the Oakes, Philip was asked to their house quite often and envied them their

"YOU DON'T SAY SO . ."

Mrs. Hesketh didn't like the idea of the telephone at first. She said so. You should hear her now—at her age—ringing up to arrange Bridge, ringing her dressmaker and her hairdresser, *and* her beauty specialist, ringing all her friends just to say how do you do, as she puts it, and going on to say a good deal more. What *would* she do without the telephone ? . . . "and such a boon in wet weather, my dear ! "

It was her eldest son who filled in that Inquiry Form. There's one alongside for you.

SEND FOR THE TELEPHONE BOOKLET—FREE

INQUIRY FORM
To the Secretary, General Post Office, London
Please send me, without any obligation on my part, a free copy of the Telephone Booklet.

Name . . . . (Mr., Mrs. or Miss)
Address . . . .
Town . . . .

An advertisement of the Post Office Telephone Service

52 Telephones were now accepted as part of middle-class life. Here is an advertisement from 1930.

refrigerator humming in the kitchen and the electric fire burning at full blast instead of the single red bar with which my mother tried to warm her bedroom.

It is hard to evaluate the world of the new housing estate in this decade. For many, it must have brought comfort and a certain status. The telephone, the Hoover, electricity were all major improvements on what had gone before. For others, this new status seems to have merely brought new fears and insecurities. Both John Osborne and George Orwell saw these fears as the predominant mood. Philip Oakes is more charitable and found some warmth both in his own home and among the children of his neighbours.

Nancy Sharman (b. 1925)

The train bore me away, through the monstrous scenery of slagheaps, chimneys, piled scrap iron, foul canals, paths of cindery mud crisscrossed by the prints of clogs. This was March, but the weather had been horribly cold and everywhere there were mounds of blackened snow. As we moved slowly through the outskirts of the town we passed row after row of little grey slum houses running at right angles to the embankment. At the back of one of the houses a young woman was kneeling on the stones, poking a stick up the leaden waste-pipe which ran from the sink inside and which I suppose was blocked. I had time to see everything about her — her sacking apron, her clumsy clogs, her arms reddened by the cold. She looked up as the train passed and I was almost near enough to catch her eye. She had a round pale face, the usual exhausted face of the slum girl who is twenty-five and looks forty, thanks to miscarriages and drudgery; and it wore, for the second in which I saw it, the most desolate, hopeless expression I had ever seen. It struck me that we are mistaken when we say 'It isn't the same for them as it would be for us', and that people bred in the slums can imagine nothing but the slums. For what I saw in her face was not the ignorant suffering of an animal. She knew well enough what was happening to her — understood as well as I did what a dreadful destiny it was to be kneeling there in the bitter cold, on the slimy stones of a slum backyard, poking a stick up a foul drain-pipe.

This famous extract from George Orwell's *Road to Wigan Pier* is echoed in one of the most lively and vivid accounts of working-class life in the thirties, Nancy Sharman's *Nothing to Steal*. Nancy Sharman was brought up in Northam, a working-class area of Southampton, hemmed in by railways, the docks and the gasworks. Her father was a boss stevedore at the docks, the man who collected a team of dockers to unload the ships as they came in. He was, however, a violent and brutal man, spending much of his earnings on drink, and then bullying or neglecting his family.

The real heroine of the book is Nancy's mother, "the most beautiful woman in the world," remembers her daughter. "Apart from her supreme gentleness she had more guts than anybody else that I ever knew and her fortitude in adversity was magnificent." It needed to be. Life with Nancy's father was so unsettled that Nancy had known eleven different homes and six different schools by the time she was seven. The family used to hire a handcart at sixpence an hour to move around their possessions. Nancy's father died of drink when she was seven and it was discovered that, as he had never paid any insurance stamps, there was no widow's

53 Despite all the new building, living conditions in many areas remained appalling. A backyard, 1937.

54 Nancy Sharman's Southampton — the docks dominate the town.

pension for his wife. Nancy's mother had to work full-time as well as keep home for her three children. She was helped by her brother, "Uncle Joe", who came to live with the family, though he, like so many others at the time, was unemployed.

The house they lived in had two living rooms, a kitchen and three bedrooms. There always had to be lodgers with them, at one time a family with two children. There was little furniture. The floor was covered by lino, scrubbed every day by Nancy's mother, until its pattern had completely disappeared.

The only furnishings the kitchen boasted were a black iron gas stove, supplied by the gas company which was then privately owned, a small table on which Mum kept her pots and pans and a washing bowl, and a gas boiler which stood next to the gas stove. Apart from the kitchen sink and drainer, that was all there was.

There was no bathroom in the house and every Saturday night all the pots, pans and kettles were filled with water which was heated for the tin bath. The family would go in one after the other, with Uncle Joe, perhaps wisely, going out to the Public Baths. Finally, all the coloured clothes were washed in the bath

water, Nancy's mother working until the early hours to get everything finished.

The continual battle to keep the house and family clean dominated life. The coal for heating arrived each week and was stored under the stairs, leaving dust everywhere. Even outside, the coal dust covered everything, from washing left out to dry to babies put out in their prams. Inside the homes, fleas, bedbugs and mice were the enemies. Beds had to be continually searched for bugs which, if undetected, would come out to feed on those asleep, leaving nasty red

55 Albert Smith, unemployed, January 1939. Benefit for a family of six is £2.7.6 a week.

sores. Nancy's mother became an expert at killing mice with a poker as they ran across the living room.

Northam was a poor community and there really was "nothing to steal" from the homes, so no one bothered to lock them. The children learned quickly how to survive. The local bakery would sell from its back door bread which was no longer fresh enough to sell in the shops and so this was the best place to buy it. At the local markets it was always best to wait until the end of the day when what was left over was sold off cheaply. Uncle Joe would smuggle in odds and ends from the docks and the family kitchen ended up painted the same colour as the funnels of the Cunard liners.

The only charity the family received was from the meals centre.

At Northam, there was a meals centre for children in dire need. They came from all over Southampton. . . . Breakfast was at eight o'clock and consisted of half a slice of bread and margarine and half a slice of bread and jam with a mug of cocoa. This was served on Monday, Wednesday and Friday mornings. On the other days, breakfast consisted of a bowl of very thin porridge or watery milk and a slice of bread. Dinners were more varied, with lots of potatoes and minced meat . . . on two days a week there were apples or oranges as extras, given out instead of pudding. This was the highlight of the free meals for many. I think there must have been some two hundred who attended this meals centre.

The children also attended a variety of churches, partly to get them out of the house, but also to gain tickets for Christmas parties.

Northam was, of course, a community with its own pastimes, traditions and loyalties. A favourite weekend activity for the community was ratting. Rats were captured and put in cages, then those with dogs were assembled and the rats were let out to a certain and horrible fate. Any who escaped the dogs were beaten to death by the surrounding crowds. Occasionally, Northam was invaded by gangs from other areas and all the local boys would arm themselves with sticks, stones and

dustbin lids to fight off the intruders. There were also more sober gatherings. There was a night of open-air dancing every New Year's Eve and major events such as George VI's Coronation in 1937 were celebrated in style.

In Guildford Street, [Nancy remembers] we had a tremendous party, with everybody's kitchen tables and chairs in a long line down the middle of the road. The houses were festooned with flags and bunting, and we all wore red, white and blue, even if only in the form of a ribbon. . . . We Northamites danced and sang to accordions, banjoes, and even a piano which someone had got out on the pavement . . . it was indeed a grand and memorable day. The old

56 Children wait outside Hoxton Market Mission for a meal.

enjoyed it as much as the young, who went to bed tired but happy. It was our King and Queen; they belonged to us as much as we belonged to them. We were British and proud of it.

57 The Coronation of George VI, 1937. Celebrations are held in local communities throughout Britain. Here is a street party in Lancashire.

Gradually, the outside world began to penetrate Northam. The cinema arrived, of course, bringing a new world of glamour. Nancy wanted to be a film dancing star when she grew up and got her Uncle Joe to make her only pair of shoes into tap-dancing ones. Then there was the arrival of the wireless in Nancy's home.

Uncle Joe bought a wireless from Curry's for some money down and then an instalment of sixpence a week. Our excitement was truly electric! Mum had a pink glow to her cheeks. . . . Joe unwrapped the shiny black and white set and shushed us while he read the instructions. . . . One end of the sideboard was cleared and the wireless was placed on it as reverently as if it had been the Crown Jewels. . . . I made a cover for

the wireless from an old dressing gown, and it was religiously covered up when not in use . . . only Mum and Uncle Joe were allowed to touch it. We were indeed entering the electric age.

By the late thirties, there were more ominous signs of change. At school, the children were told that

a train would be arriving at Southampton packed with children from Spain, mostly orphans, or children who had been separated from their parents when fleeing from Franco.

The children were asked to gather any food or gifts they could and be at the station to hand them over to the Spanish refugees. Nancy's mother collected three paper bags full of food.

We Southampton children eagerly reached up to the windows along the whole length of the train and the excited Spanish children clutched our remarkable assortment of bags, all the while gabbling away in their, to us, incomprehensible language. Mum's three bags and half of the sweets disappeared through one compartment window and the rest of the sweets through the next. Some of the Spanish children looked bewildered and some of them seemed to have been crying, but many of them were smiling and I knew that they were saying 'thank you, thank you,' in their own language. The train did not stay for very long, and, as it moved off, we all waved furiously to each other until it had gone out of sight.

In the summer of 1939, Nancy's mother decided that she could afford the ten shillings charge to send Nancy off to a holiday camp. The activities at the camp were hardly what Nancy expected.

It was June 1939 but I was oblivious to the world situation. However, its seriousness was becoming increasingly apparent. On our third day in Camp, all of us girls were assembled and were told that the King and Queen would like us to do some very important work for them. We were taken to some huts in coaches and there confronted with strange grey and black rubber objects with round filter discs. We had to put a rubber band round the disc to attach it to the mask-piece. They were called gas-masks . . . instead of teaching us about how one fifth of the

58 Refugees from Spain. 4,200 children were on this liner which arrived in Southampton in 1937.

world was red [this was the colour of the British Empire on the map] and British, we should have been taught something about Hitler, Mussolini and their kind.

Two months later Britain was at war.

Nothing to Steal is a remarkable story. It shows how little state support was given to those in need and how much a family depended on its own strengths to survive. The courage and determination of Nancy's mother, despite continual ill-health and the crushing weight of the poverty and dirt of Northam, were vital for the family. Many cannot have been so lucky.

3 SEPTEMBER 1939

We believed we were ready for the news, however bad it might be, but it was still a shock one Sunday morning when I went into the dining room to find my mother lying on the couch while from the radio behind her an old man's voice, as dry and punctilious as my Uncle Arthur's, told us that we were at war with Germany. (Philip Oakes, *From Middle England*)

Neville Chamberlain, Prime Minister:

I am speaking to you from the Cabinet Room at 10, Downing Street.

This morning the British Ambassador in Berlin handed the German Government a final note stating that unless we heard from them by 11 o'clock that they were prepared to withdraw their troops from Poland a state of war would exist between us.

I have to tell you now that no such undertaking has been received and consequently this country is at war with Germany.

Extract from Harold Nicolson's diary, 3 September:

At 1.50 I motor down with Victor Cazelet to Sissinghurst. There are many army lorries passing along the road and a few pathetic trucks

59 Call-up. Men from the Territorial Army assemble as Britain prepares for war, September 1939.

evacuating East End refugees. In one of these there is an elderly woman who shakes her fist at us and shouts that it is all the fault of the rich . . .

Instead of teaching us about how one fifth of the world was red and British, we should have been taught something about Hitler, Mussolini and their kind. (Nancy Sharman, *Nothing to Steal*)

60 "We should have been taught something about Hitler, Mussolini and their kind." (Nancy Sharman). British school children concentrate on Britain – a geography lesson in a Yorkshire village school in the 1930s.

DATE LIST

1929

May — General Election. The Labour Party emerges as the largest party.

June — Ramsay MacDonald becomes Prime Minister in a Labour Government.

October — The Wall Street Crash sets off a worldwide depression.

November — Unemployment in Britain reaches 1,325,000.

1930

April — Unemployment in Britain passes 2,000,000.

May — The Cabinet rejects Oswald Mosley's proposals for reducing unemployment. Mosley resigns his post in the Government.

June — The Simon Report on India – the Report recommends greater Indian participation in government.

November — First Round Table Conference on India in London.

December — Unemployment reaches 2,500,000.

1931

February — Oswald Mosley, having left the Labour Party, announces he will set up a New Party.

July — Unemployment reaches 2,800,000.

August — The May Committee, which has been set up by the Government to consider government spending, calls for cuts in spending and higher taxation. The Labour Cabinet is split on how to make cuts and foreign money is increasingly withdrawn from London.
MacDonald finally decides he will form a National Government of all those who are prepared to support a programme of recovery which will include cuts. Most Labour Members refuse to support him.

September — The new National Government announces cuts in the salaries of all public employees including teachers and the armed services. There is a mutiny in the Navy at Invergordon. More money is withdrawn from London and the Government takes Britain off the Gold Standard.
Second Round Table Conference on the future of India. This conference is attended by Gandhi.

October — General Election. MacDonald and his supporters win 556 seats, the Labour Party only 46. The new Government is, in fact, dominated by Conservatives and remains so until the end of the decade. Mosley's New Party is heavily defeated and is soon disbanded.

November — Statute of Westminster. Gives the Dominions, Australia, New Zealand, Canada and Australia, complete freedom from British Parliamentary control.

1932

February — Disarmament Conference opens in Geneva. It continues until late 1933 but makes little progress.

October — Mosley launches the British Union of Fascists.

1933

January — Unemployment reaches three million. Hitler comes to power in Germany.

1934

January — The economic recovery is under way. Unemployment down to 2,400,000.
The Unemployment Act standardizes benefits for the nation but is hotly attacked for reducing some local benefits.
The Distressed Areas Act provides some, but not substantial, help for depressed areas.

June — The great fascist meeting at Olympia ends in violence and starts the decline of British fascism.

1935

January — Unemployment 2,290,000.
The Government of India Act is passed after a long struggle. Allows for greater participation by Indians in government.

March — A Government White Paper (statement) on defence sees Germany as a possible future enemy. Hitler announces in the same month that Germany has an air force and will bring in conscription to rebuild her army.

May — George V celebrates his Jubilee, twenty-five years on the throne.

June — Ramsay MacDonald resigns as Prime Minister. He is succeeded by Stanley Baldwin.
Anglo-German Naval Agreement. Britain agrees that Germany may start to rebuild her Navy.
Peace Ballot. A house-to-house survey shows that the vast majority of those asked support the League of Nations and back its use of sanctions against aggressors.

October — Mussolini invades Abyssinia. The League of Nations backs sanctions but these are not complete and have no major effect.

November — General Election. The National Government wins 431 seats, the Labour Party recovers to 154 seats but is still far behind.

December — The British Foreign Minister, Samuel Hoare, and his French counterpart, Pierre Laval, make an agreement that Mussolini will be able to keep part of his conquests. There is a major outcry in protest in Britain. Hoare resigns and Britain is, in general, discredited.

1936	
January	Unemployment 2,130,000.
	George V dies, and is succeeded by his son, Edward VIII.
	Public Order Act. Restricts the right to demonstrate.
March	Hitler sends troops into the Rhineland. Britain makes no effective protest.
July	Spanish Civil War begins. Britain decides on a policy of non-intervention.
December	Abdication crisis. Edward abdicates after the Government refuses to accept Mrs Simpson as Queen. He is succeeded by his brother, the Duke of York, now George VI.

1937	
January	Unemployment down to 1,670,000.
	Defence spending for 1936-7 is £186 million (up from £103 million in 1932-3).
May	Coronation of George VI. Baldwin retires. Neville Chamberlain takes over as Prime Minister.

1938	
February	Anthony Eden resigns as Foreign Secretary in disagreement with the policy of negotiation with the fascist dictators.
April	Hitler annexes Austria.
September	Crisis over Czechoslovakia as Hitler demands the right to incorporate the German-speaking population on the western frontier into Germany. Britain and France agree, at the Munich Agreement, that he may do so.

1939	
March	Hitler takes over the remainder of Czechoslovakia. The British policy of "appeasement" is in ruins. Chamberlain announces that Britain will guarantee the borders of Poland against German attack.
April	Conscription is reintroduced in Britain.
May	Hitler and Mussolini, already collaborators, make a military alliance – the Pact of Steel.
August	Germany and Russia sign a non-aggression pact. Poland is now isolated.
1 September	Hitler invades Poland.
3 September	Britain and France declare war on Germany.

BOOKS FOR FURTHER READING

General

R. Blythe, *The Age of Illusion* (Oxford University Press, 1983) Essays on events and personalities of the 1920s and 1930s.

S. Constantine, *Unemployment in Britain between the Wars* (Longmans Seminar Series, 1980) Includes extracts from documents of the period.

C. Cook and J. Stevenson, *The Slump* (Quartet Books, 1979) Excellent study of political developments during the decade.

M. Howard, *War and the Liberal Conscience* (Oxford University Press, 1981) The chapters on the 1930s look at the dilemmas facing those who wished to preserve peace.

S. Hynes, *The Auden Generation* (Faber Paperbacks, 1979) An excellent study of the relationship between literature and politics.

P. Kennedy, *The Realities Behind Diplomacy* (Allen and Unwin/Fontana, 1981) The chapters on the 1930s look at the pressures which influenced defence and foreign policy.

C. Mowat, *Britain between the Wars* (Methuen, 1968) Although thirty years old, still one of the best introductions to the period.

H. Nicolson, *Diaries and Letters 1930-39* (Collins, 1966; a shortened version in Penguin) Gives an excellent view of the social and political life of the upper middle classes.

Robert Rhodes James, *The British Revolution* (Methuen, 1978) Concentrates on Parliamentary life and is especially good on the debates on defence.

J. Stevenson, *Britain 1914-45*
(Pelican Social History of Britain, 1984)

A.J.P. Taylor, *English History 1914-45* (Penguin, 1970) Good general overview of social and political developments.

F. Williams, *A Pattern of Rulers* (Longmans, 1965) A series of essays on leading figures of the day. Very good on Baldwin and Chamberlain.

Individual Politicians

Baldwin:

R. Middlemas and J. Barnes, *Baldwin* (Weidenfeld and Nicolson, 1969) A very long and detailed biography.

H. Montgomery Hyde, *Baldwin* (Hart Davis, 1973).

K. Young, *Baldwin* (Weidenfeld and Nicolson, 1976) A good introduction.

Bevan:

M. Foot, *Aneurin Bevan*, Volume I (Paladin, 1975) A very lively biography.

J. Lee, *My Life with Nye* (Penguin, 1981) Excellent picture of Bevan by his widow.

Mosley:

N. Mosley, *Rules of the Game* and *Beyond the Pale* (Fontana, 1982) An excellent life of Mosley by his son.

R. Skidelsky, *Oswald Mosley* (Papermac, 1980) The best general study of Mosley, his ideas and his impact.

Chamberlain:

H. Montgomery Hyde, *Chamberlain* (Weidenfeld and Nicolson, 1976)

Churchill:

M. Gilbert, *The Wilderness Years* (Macmillan, 1981) A study of Churchill in the 1930s.

M. Gilbert, *Churchill. A Photographic Portrait* (Heinemann, 1984)
(Martin Gilbert is also writing the official biography of Churchill, Volume V of which covers these years).

Writers

Virginia Woolf:

Q. Bell, *Virginia Woolf* (The Hogarth Press, 1972) The best biography.

J. Lehmann, *Virginia Woolf and her World* (Thames and Hudson, 1975).

M. Rosenthal, *Virginia Woolf* (Routledge and Kegan Paul, 1979) A study of Virginia Woolf's writing.

(Virginia Woolf's *Diaries* and *Letters* are published by the Hogarth Press and most of her novels and other works by Penguin.)

W.H. Auden:

The best biography is by H. Carpenter (Allen and Unwin, 1981)

George Orwell:

The best biography is by Bernard Crick (Secker and Warburg, 1981). See also *Orwell Remembered* (Ariel Books, 1984)
(George Orwell's novels and his *Road to Wigan Pier* are in Penguin.)

"The People"

R. Rhodes James (Editor), *Chips. The Diaries of Sir Henry Channon* (Weidenfeld and Nicolson, 1967; also in Penguin)

R. Cobb, *Still Life* (Chatto and Windus, 1983)

P. Oakes, *From Middle England, A Memory of the Thirties* (Andre Deutsch, 1980; also, with the second volume of his life, in Penguin)

J. Osborne, *A Better Class of Person* (Faber and Faber, 1981)

N. Sharman, *Nothing to Steal* (Kaye and Ward, 1977)

(For working-class life see also W. Greenwood, *Love on the Dole*, Penguin, 1969)

INDEX